Presented To:

_____

From:

_____

Date:

_____

Message:

_____

_____

_____

_____

_____

_____

THE GOLDEN GOOSE
MASTERS SELLING

Proven Methods That Will Grow Your Sales Exponentially

By Grant Senzani

Reviews

"Grant has written a relatable and practical book that is based on real-life experiences and provides solutions that would benefit a business owner, salesperson or anyone looking to start a side hustle. This book will provide you with insights on how to sell, relate better to your prospects, and inject personality and belief in your pitch."

Bongane Shabalala
– Entrepreneur and Business Owner

"The book gives great insight into the technical aspects of selling. Technical, as in, the mathematics of selling. What I liked the most about this book is that it shows the reader exactly how to measure their success in the marketing/selling journey. It is one thing to stand in front of people and sell; it is another to be able to measure your impact and I think this book is great for highlighting that."

Akhona Monakali
– Entrepreneur and Business Owner

"'*The Golden Goose Masters Selling*' is an enlightening book for anybody looking to improve or revive their sales skills. Using his own experiences, Grant shares relevant moments at the beginning of each chapter that one can relate to. One can apply these lessons in one's own experiences in life, work, and business. This is a book I will often refer to on my business journey for building real relationships with my clients."

Nigel Sibisi
– Entrepreneur and Creative Consultant

"This is a life manual, not just a book about sales. It teaches you how to raise your belief on the products/services you offer to clients and opens up your mind to the possibilities of running your own successful business."

Osvaldo Antonio Nhaca
– Human Behaviours Researcher,
Mental Health Consultant and Public Speaker

"An interesting perspective and a fresh outlook on existing fundamentals of sales. A fun, funny and practical read. The author's personal experiences make the science behind sales relatable. Grant is an incredibly perspicacious author. After reading this book, you'll be sold on selling!"

Banele Masobela
– Mompreneur and Business Owner

"I was up at 2 A.M. reading this book. I'm blown away by its practicality! I also loved how it highlighted various points from belief to the actual sale! My biggest takeaway? The importance of believing in your product/service"

Sibusiso Mahlangu
– Perfumer, Entrepreneur and Open Format DJ

Dedication

To everyone who finds joy in selling, not because it is
the only job they could find, but rather because selling
is part of the fibre of their being.

My advice? Keep selling. May this book help you to do
so exponentially.

Acknowledgements

To Jacques Janneke and Ernst Wilkins.

My love for sales is because you two were willing to share all you knew.

Thank you.

FOREWORD

I remember my first job in sales, yes – sales is a real job. I was part of the fortunate few who chose to go into sales because I was inspired and empowered that I too could make phenomenal sales. Many find themselves in sales by default i.e. they left Matric, did not know what to do and the only available jobs, where work experience was not required, were sales positions. Out of this choice, many will hate it and vow never to return but many will love it until death they do part. Whether you fall in the love or hate spectrum, this book is about to revolutionise your world and make you either fall in love with sales or make you want to up your game.

It does not matter what product or service you are selling; most of the work must go into yourself, your beliefs, and your intellect. After all, you are first and foremost the product, because the reality is that people buy from people. When I considered the title of this book, it made sense that as a sales executive for most of my working career, this is a book I need on my shelf. However, I wish I had read this as part of my high school syllabus. This book sets foundational principles not just for sales but for life. I believe that selling or anything you do must be connected to a higher calling. Yes please, let us make a profit and a success, but may the hunger for money come second to a hunger to make a difference and an impact in the world. When our motive is to make a difference, our attitude and aptitude take us to a newer and higher dimension of thinking. This in turn changes the way we do things, the things we say and the way we conduct ourselves. Don't you want people to walk away from your meeting and say, "Wow, I don't even feel like he/she was trying to sell to me? Instead, they cared about my business, they listened and addressed the problem and offered a solution." That's when you have become more than just a salesperson, but a person on a mission to make the world a little better. This is who Grant is; a man on a mission to make the world a better place through living his dream.

When I met Grant through my mentors, I met him in the confines of Toastmasters. Secondly, I heard that he had written a book and was breaking out into the publishing space. It was purely based on his relationship with my mentors and the evidence of their genuine relationship that I knew that he would be the publisher of my book as well, which he is. Grant lives sales. The success of Brad and my book can easily be attributed to his constant marketing and sales advice, which was made up of identifying the target audience, choosing the right cover, our social media presence and just his consistent voice and support in the life of our book even up until today. Grant believes that our success is also his success, which it is, because that's ownership and sales is ownership, even after the sale is done.

I love the style in which this book was written, it not only holds pertinent information for success, but you can see and hear Grant in the chapters, whether he is being serious or quirky. He also bares himself in the book, by sharing his learnings, failures, and successes. Grant is his own product and some of his traits have been branded by the people whom he has impacted; they endearingly call him "The man with the Velvet Voice."

Whether you are selling a tangible product, a service or selling yourself in an interview, this handbook will assist you to put your best foot forward, avoid the hurdles and overtake your peers. It must be the handbook for every salesperson looking to become a master at selling. Its information can be trusted because it has been lived by the author himself. Grant is always looking to do better and refine all that he does, so I know that these principles have been tried and tested at least more than once. I hope you will enjoy the book as much as I have and find the information useful for daily application.

Mandy Petrus
— Author of Believe Again and Avid Salesperson

OTHER BOOKS
BY GRANT SENZANI

When the Golden Goose Doesn't Lay Eggs
Lessons on Fulfilling Your Potential

The Golden Goose Becomes an Authorpreneur
Proven Hacks to Self-Publishing Within a Year

CONTENTS

HI, I AM GRANT...

It is 2007 and I have just arrived in Pretoria, South Africa coming from a two-year academic streak of failure from the University of Namibia. If I had returned to Namibia, I would have been academically excluded. My parents do not know this though. In their minds, I am looking for a better university – one that is more recognised than the University of Namibia. Although the idea had merit; it was not the complete truth. Shame on me - I know!

The time I spent in Namibia was a tug-of-war between academics and the cool life. Instead of diligently studying and at least passing a few of my computer engineering modules, I discovered women and partying. Those two usually do not get along with academics. The tug-of-war regarding academic success versus academic failure was pretty much one-sided. Before you continue to judge me, I would like you to know that not all was lost. I learnt how to rap and I showcased some of my songs on a few stages. I was also on the radio a few times, for interviews and rap freestyles. My cool points were on a Mount Everest high and at the other end of the seesaw, my academic achievements were Dead Sea low.

I am 19 in the year 2007 and will be taking a gap year, only to start studying again in 2008 and will be 20 in my first year. Where did the time go? 13 years later at the time of the writing of this book, I still ask myself that question.

Deep insecurities are coming to the surface like bubbles in the water. The counterparts that I studied with at the University of Namibia are all looking to finish their qualifications in 2009. When I do the maths that means that I will only be in the second year of my university studies. I also know my classmates from Varsity College Pretoria will all be much younger than me. It is crazy. I know it is said that we should not compare ourselves with other people, but we all know that ensuring that you know what is out there helps you to set a standard or remove it completely. My standard had been set by all the classmates I geographically left behind in Namibia.

2007, will play a significant role in the next ten years of my life. It is the year that I picked up a book that changed and fine-tuned my mentality towards my life and ambitions. Initially, I thought it made sense for me to climb the academic ladder first, and thereafter, find a job and do the same ladder climbing in the corporate environment. I would then buy a property and earn some passive income, eventually get married, have children, and keep working until I cannot work any further.

The book I read challenged that idea and shook that dream at its foundation. It tapped past the ideas I had for my life and went straight to my soul. It taught me that we are truly the architects of our destinies and do not have to follow a script, or better articulated "the" script. You know, the script that our society and family hand us? The book was by Robert Kiyosaki called, "*Rich Dad, Poor Dad.*" It spoke of entrepreneurship as a possible option. As I read through the chapters of the book, I would reminisce of times I had ideas but never pursued them or was ignorant about what I was onto.

At 12 years old, I tried starting a babysitter's club. I looked for a few mothers that I knew and sent them an introduction letter. The letter let these mothers know about my new business and how it could help them. That business failed. The lesson I learnt from my attempt was that some mothers would prefer to torture their children by taking them to malls or even worse, banks! On a more serious note, however, I learnt that doing your research beforehand is an advantage – a huge one.

That same year I tried selling popcorn outside our electric gate. Selling popcorn in an up-market suburb did not work as well as I thought it would. I learnt that people in the suburbs do not buy popcorn off the street or from their neighbours. As a result, that venture failed but in return, I had learnt about having the right target audience and looking for a product that suits their needs.

Later that year, I learnt how to make a soil bed from school and decided to create my own garden. My brother, Aubrey, was my first investor. He bought the cabbage and spinach seeds. My sister, Khangeziwe, and I would then till the ground and plant the seeds once the soil was ready. That venture highlighted my lack of patience. I could not wait for the seeds to emanate from the ground. My mum took advantage of this and kept the spoils – the cabbage and spinach heads that my sister and I had planted. I do not judge her; I would have done the same thing in her shoes. Looking back, I should have also thought to sell the business to my mum to pay back my investor and fellow worker for the hard work put in.

The last venture that I will mention was with a friend. We were going to pitch an idea to the

Namibian Broadcasting Corporation (NBC). They had ads on repeat that captured how important it was to pay your television license. I noticed, however, that they did not have a child in any of their broadcasts at the time, so I thought, "Hey, why not have a child in the advert? They enjoy television the most! Perhaps I should show a child having fun while watching television, then we take away the television set and all the furniture (the punishment for not having paid a television license) and then show the child watching the wall. Great idea Grant!" Enthused by my idea, I called my friend Musangi aka "Moose" to help me. He was interested in doing a shoot and I was interested in making money so naturally, I thought, "Now is the time! He gets what he wants, and I get what I want. Win/win? Yip! Win/win!" I called Moose and he agreed. Now I had to move to step two.

Step two had me looking for a child that was interested in playing the character that we wished to showcase. The child I had picked was also cute and I knew that he would make this work. I got consent from his parents then Moose and I were good to go. A day later, we shot the scenes and then Moose went to work with editing the video. He called me a few days later when the video clip was ready. Excitement filled my veins! My idea had become our idea, and our idea was gaining traction.

I called the NBC and asked to talk to a head honcho. They gave me his line and I am not too sure what my 16-year-old-self told him but before you knew it, he said yes to a meeting and gave us a date to deliver a presentation. My voice had just broken, and I sounded like a drum on steroids, this I believe was the edge that sealed the deal. Looking back, my deep voice had always played a role in instilling confidence and authority even if I did not know what I was talking about.

Moose and I arrived at the meeting both wearing jeans and t-shirts in a room filled with adults dressed in formal attire. We were asked to present and within a matter of minutes we shared what their gap was, then presented the solution by showing them the clip. They loved it! When we concluded the meeting, they mentioned that they would get back to us. Every entrepreneur knows what that means – waiting.

Frustrated from waiting, I called the head honcho later that same week to ask him what the next step was. He mentioned that the clip was too long and would cost too much to air on television. This news upset me and seeing that I did not know how to handle objections, I agreed. Deal lost and money lost. Experienced gained and lesson learnt.

In retrospect, I realised that the problem was that I did not understand selling. By selling I mean, the giving or handing over of a product or service in exchange for money. Yes, they may have not been the target market, yes, I may have not persevered long enough or known how to handle objections, but the root of these problems was that I did not know how to sell. You can have an extraordinary talent and people could beckon for you every chance they get to, but if you do not know how to sell, you can forget about ensuring that you create a secondary income or create any income at all. Selling is vital to your actualised products and services like blood is to the body or air is to your lungs.

Years have passed and ideas have come and gone. Some went well, others failed. Experience gained; lessons learnt. My most recent achievement has been the self-publishing of my first book, *When the Golden Goose Doesn't Lay Eggs: Lessons on Fulfilling Your Potential.* It has sold well, for a new entrant in the literary market. I was also able to get it featured at the 2018 Kingsmead Book Festival.

Why write this book on sales? Things are beginning to go well for me from a business point of view when it comes to sales. As I mentioned it was not always like this. Writing this book allowed me to begin to map out how I got to this point. I hope that you will learn from my mistakes and implement the frameworks and points that I share with you. I hope that your sales process will become steady and thereafter become exponential.

I have broken this book up into three sections:

1. Before the Sale
2. During the Sale
3. After the Sale

These sections will help you find a process to work on until it becomes a system that is dependable and will give you the returns that you seek.

The frameworks that I will share with you are:

1. The Belief Matrix ©

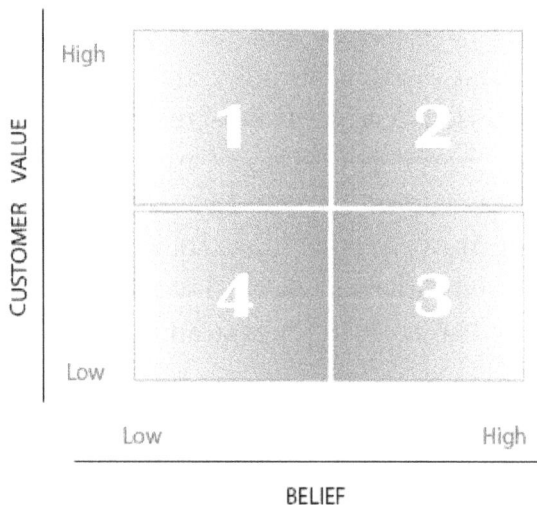

Figure 1 The Belief Matrix ©

2. The Sales Wheel of Insight ©

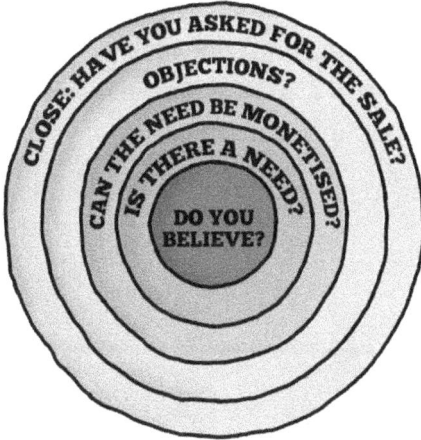

Figure 2 The Sales Wheel of Insight ©

3. The Questions Loop ©

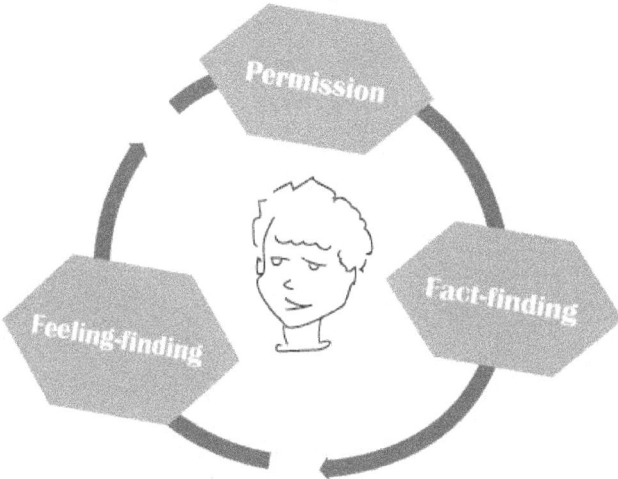

Figure 3 The Questions Loop ©

The ideas in those frameworks are not unique. My expression of them birthed by experience, however, is. If they work for you, my job is done. If they do not my job is done, because that is one less way to get to where you want to go.

Enjoy the read and the growth that it will come with.

BEFORE
THE SALE

Selling starts once you have initiated contact with your prospect, not a moment later than that. You may think that it is when you physically meet, but that initial contact, whether that is via email or phone or at a networking event, this is where the sale begins. The mistake that most salespeople make is that they believe that the sale begins after the initial contact – after they have made the call and have set a date to meet up. This is something that Marco Jacobs, founder of M3C Consulting, shared with me. As a fellow entrepreneur, he was vehement about this point when I met with him. He mentioned how you should be in good stead from the get-go because every bit of influence will count towards the sale. The influence may start small but after some time it will grow and that mountain of influence will cascade into decisions swaying your way.

This was evident to me when I met with prospects that had Googled who I was and knew what I did before our meeting. Having a meeting with them is their way of seeing if who I am online correlates with who I am in person.

To further add to Marco's advice, I would also like to propose that the sale starts in the mind of the salesperson as a thought. The thought of a sale then propels you to contact the prospective client. Your belief here is paramount as this starts the process. From experience I can tell you this much, with no belief there will be no sale. The higher the belief of the sale going through, however, the higher the chances of selling.

The question is: do you believe?

CHAPTER 1
DO YOU BELIEVE?

There is an iconic scene in The Matrix when Neo, the main character played by Keanu Reeves, is in a downtown subway at a telephone booth holding the receiver of a public phone, which had been shattered by a bullet, shot across from him by Agent Smith. This call that had been disturbed, was vital. It would have teleported him from the matrix into the real-world and saved him from the dreaded Agent Smith, played by Hugo Weaving, the antagonist whose mission is to kill Neo.

As Agent Smith begins to approach Neo, Neo begins to run out of the subway station but suddenly comes to a halt. He then turns around and decides to rather fight Agent Smith. Up to this point in the movie, no one had faced an agent and won, but Neo decides to challenge that dogma and gets into a battle with Agent Smith.

Meanwhile, in the real-world Morpheus, his mentor, and Trinity (soon to be lover) are watching anxiously on the monitors. When they see Neo stop and turn around to fight Agent Smith, Trinity asks Morpheus, "What is he doing?" Morpheus responds, "He is beginning to believe."

Belief is defined as trust, faith, or confidence in someone or something. Why is belief so important? How does this apply to you? It is important because belief induces us to act and gives us certain results. In Neo's case, his belief led him to fight Agent Smith, which led to a temporary win as a result. In your case, belief could lead you to sell your product or service. If you cannot sell your product/service to someone, you must first ask yourself whether you believe in your product/service. Well, do you?

I believe that we can only sell what we believe is best for the recipient of our product/service. When we do, there is an authenticity that seeps out of our aura that people are attracted to. People will be less reluctant to buy something that you believe would be of great value for them. This would stem from the authenticity and conviction that would aid you in persuading someone to buy your product/service.

We all, however, know of some salespeople that do otherwise and sell to only reach their quota. Sooner rather than later, that comes to an end. Customers will catch on that you just want to make a quick buck at their expense and will refuse to exchange their hard-earned money just to make sure you reach your monthly quota.

Belief breeds action that, in turn, gives you results. Therefore, within the Sales Wheel of Insight, belief is the focal point. Without belief, the whole sales process comes to halt or you become a victim of stunted results.

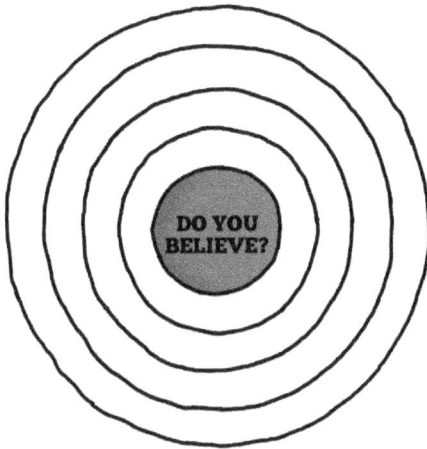

Figure 4 - The Sales Wheel of Insight © - Belief

The following are great questions to ask and carefully consider:

1. Do you believe in your product/service?
2. Do you believe that it is what is best for the client?

In light of this, I have made, what I dub, The Matrix of Belief© and it paints four different outcomes which depend on your belief and the belief you have in the value of your product for customers.

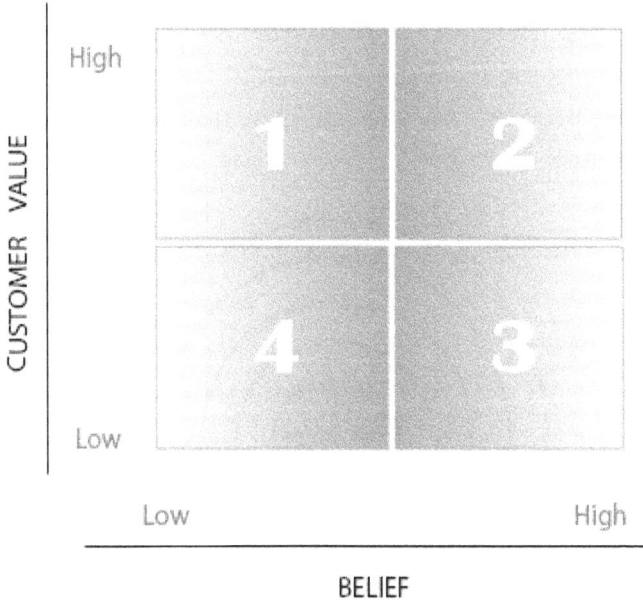

Figure 5: The Matrix of Belief ©

1. I do not believe in my service and/or product although I believe it would be good for the customer.

There are products/services I do not believe in but are great for certain clients. These types of products/services do not serve my needs and therefore, I am biased towards them. I may sell advertising space to a client who really needs it and believes in its power, even though I may not see how this would translate into solid benefits for them.

For a long time, I felt this way about Facebook and YouTube ad services. I did not believe in them and if I were working on selling those services, I would have had a tough time because I know for a fact that I did not believe in them. A prospect would, however, see the need and buy regardless of my disbelief in the service.

I would still encourage sales like this for only one reason: it is not about me or you, it is about the client and what they want. If they believe in your product/service, even when you do not, and know that it will certainly add value to them, then sell away. I know the amount of hesitation you will feel. I have felt it before. Keep in the forefront that this is about the buyer and not yourself. Just be sure to share your opinions and leave the final choice with your prospect.

Lastly, if you do not believe in your product/service ensure that you have a solution. Do not let that customer just walk away. You are there to provide a solution for your prospect's needs.

On one winter evening, Anna and I decided to visit a Spur. We were met at the door by a waiter named Jabu. Jabu was an enthusiastic and helpful waiter bringing as much positivity to the table as he could. Like all waiters, he handed us the menu and left once he got the drinks order. Anna was feeling like having a burger and I was prepared to engulf Spur's tortillas.

When the waiter returned with our drinks, Rooibos with honey and lemon, he then asked what we would like to eat. Now, I know it is customary to ensure that you let the lady order first, but I knew Anna would ask a few questions, so I went straight into giving him my order and then let Anna order next. I promise to be more patient next time. Anna asked a few questions about the Mexicana Burger that she wanted to order. Was it a good burger? Was it ordered regularly? These were some of the questions that she asked. The waiter, after answering those questions, then mentioned what he would recommend: a burger with bacon in it rather. She looked at the menu a second time and then concluded that she would pick the Mexicana Burger and not take Jabu's advice. Jabu believed that the burger was not delicious, but Anna did, and he allowed the customer to be queen and took down the order despite his disbelief. When Anna took a bite of her burger she smiled and then said, "Jabu should recommend this burger from now on. It tastes amazing."

This is what all salespeople ought to do. Regardless of how you feel, if your prospect, after your suggestion, still decides otherwise, it is important to serve your prospect. Your job is to ensure that you share all your alternatives but fulfil your prospect's wishes.

2. *You believe in your service/product and you believe that it is in your prospect's best interest as well.*

If this is you, then you will naturally get your client to sign on the dotted line and exchange their hard-earned money for your product/service depending on how you communicate – which I will cover in another chapter. For now, you must realise how your belief will seep from you as enthusiasm which will naturally encourage your prospects.

A friend of mine, Thabang, currently works for a beer company and he strongly believes in beer. He loves it. He also believes that it is in everyone's best interest that they drink too. He says, "Beer, is nature's social lubricant." He often jokes about how you can jog without running shoes, but it is always better when you do. He mentions the same applies to alcohol, you can go to social gatherings without it, but it is always better when you do.

I do not drink alcohol anymore, so I simply laugh at his remarks and enjoy the enthusiasm and charisma that comes from his belief in his "social lubricant". But what if Thabang were to meet with someone who does drink? Think of the amount of persuasion he would have seeping from all that enthusiasm. All Thabang would need to do is communicate to that person about why buying from him would be their best solution. You can guess what the person would do, right?

Now would you sell to everyone you share this high level of enthusiasm with? No. You will, however, convert more than you would if you were in any other category.

This is the power of believing in your product/service and the good it could do for the prospect with an interest in your product/service. Sales galore!

Let us explore what would happen if you believed in your product/service but believed that it might not be in the prospect's best interest.

3. You believe in your product/service, but you do not believe that it is in the prospect's best interest.

I would advise that you approach this with caution. Remember, people can sense authenticity from a mile away. Therefore, if you happen to sell an item that they would find no value in, then you can look forward to that customer never returning. Hopefully, they do not mention that experience to anyone else because that could have negative results for your business.

Many movies and gurus make selling seem like a once-off thing. I believe that selling is not just about having someone buy something once-off and then leaving. It is about having a client want more of what you are selling. If you can read the customer's needs properly at that specific moment and in the future, then this creates an additional income stream for you. This would also mean that business could flow from referrals as well as from positive feedback from your initial client.

When I had joined Liberty Life, an insurance company, I did not believe in life cover or any other long-term insurance product. I found it exceedingly difficult to sell and even when I did, I always felt bad or would find means of getting the client to opt-out. I know, terrible on my side, but I thought that this was not in the customer's best interest, especially when it came to looking at it from a wealth-building perspective.

Being honest with your prospect about the disbelief you have with the service/product could leave you better off. Prospects can trust someone who is in their corner, cheering for them, and ensuring their needs are met. While other salespeople butter them up and look to set them up for a loss, there you will be, championing their cause. This will make you the go-to person when they need help, which ultimately means more income for you.

There are ways of ensuring that you begin to believe in your product/service. You could simply ask yourself why you do not believe in it. In most cases, you will realise that it is merely a result of information that you do not have or have never thought of. Seeking that information may give you a paradigm shift. You could get that information from clients that are adamant on having your product/service or from other people within your field.

In my case, I was always told by my manager and fellow financial advisers that I would understand the importance of long-term insurance once I got my first death claim. I never got that claim, but I did get a company that offers group schemes calling me. They mentioned that someone had passed on and had left money behind for their beneficiaries. The beneficiary, however, was still in university and was the most educated person in her family. They wanted to give her the money but preferred to work via a financial adviser who could aid her in making a good decision. I helped and this made me realise something, the money people leave behind for their beneficiaries is essential. It could ensure that their beneficiaries are never left wanting. That changed my outlook on long-term insurance.

In your case, look for stories or reasons that would help you believe that your product/service is best for your prospect. Move into the 2nd category of the Belief Matrix©. This would ensure that the only thing that would deter you from selling would simply be your communication.

Sometimes you may also conclude that your service is not the best fit for a client because it still needs to be worked on.

Take my friend, fellow entrepreneur, and founder of Von Mash, Sibusiso (S'bu) Mahlangu. He sells water and custom-made perfumes. He is now expanding into selling beard oil. S'bu is melancholy by nature and is, therefore, fixated on details. His new product, beard oils, is wanted but he feels that more work needs to be done on it. I appreciate such perfectionism but after a few laughs between us, we both agreed that releasing the beard oil while working on perfecting it would be a better alternative. That way S'bu is happy to continue working on it and the client is happy that their problem, whatever it may be, now has a solution. If you think about it deeply you would realise that S'bu would have a client that would keep buying as he is perfecting his product.

The lesson here is not to get caught up in the details to the point that you cause your potential customers to wait too long. Sell them the current product/service and when you have upgraded it, look to service your client with the upgrade. They will be happy they got the initial sale and that you thought about them when you worked on the upgrade. I would also advise you either give it to them for free or at a discount. I have seen this in my clothing business. I was not completely happy with one of the designs, but the buyer was happy to buy his hoodie regardless. I then gave him a 25% discount for the next order. He ordered another hoodie.

What happens, however, when you do not believe in your product/service and do not believe it is in your prospect's best interest?

4. **You neither believe in your service/ product nor do you believe that it is in your prospect's best interest.**

If you find yourself in this category, I suggest that you either find another job or pivot your products/services. This is the ideal answer; however, I do understand that life does not always deal us the cards we want. Life deals a certain batch and we must play our hand to the best of our ability. So, if you do not believe in your product/service then begin your self-reflective journey by asking yourself why. Why do you not believe in it? Could it be that you may feel that it is not of great quality? Does it serve a need? Do you feel that more time should be spent on improving it? If so, how would you do that, and do you have the power to make those changes? The answers to those questions should bring you the clarity to decide.

Answering all those questions is important because we all are faced with such situations, whether we are cognizant of it or not. The answers to those questions would determine whether you care about your offering and its utility to your prospect. This information is vital for your success whether in your business or your employer's business. It also allows you to mitigate any bias you may have in selling your product/service.

Lastly, the better you understand the answers to those questions, the better you will be able to serve your prospects. If you have answered all those questions and you still have the same disposition, then perhaps you ought to pivot. By pivoting I mean to seek to still give a product/service, but ensure that it is more in line with what you would like to accomplish. This is not you failing; this is you being honest with yourself and dealing with something that would potentially be a problem later.

The last reason why you must understand which category you fall under is that you should always be selling your product/service. Let people always know that you have a product/service and do not be ashamed to sell it. If you are in the 2nd category of the Belief Matrix© this will be easy, if you are in any other category, you may have some work to do. Remember products/services only get sold if they are seen. If they are not seen, then they cannot be bought. It is that simple.

Does that mean that you openly tell people that you have a product/service all the time? Well, that depends. If the atmosphere allows for it then certainly if not, however, then you would have to covertly slip it into the conversation. Be classy about it. If they bite, then speak about it. If not, then carry on as you were with your conversation. The importance of this is that you never know who will buy from you next, therefore, you should never miss out on a sales opportunity by not letting the people around you know.

When we take aspiring authors through our publishing process, one of the things we do is teach them how to develop a marketing message. This is something they should memorise and lay in wait for the opportune time to share it. Others call this an elevator pitch. Not having one of these will leave you unprepared and waffling through your products and services. Waffling seems like uncertainty and uncertainty does not translate into sales.

What would happen if you do not share at all? Allow me to share my experience with this. I was at Nedbank Toastmasters Club and I delivered a speech as per my educational requirements. I did not make mention of my book simply because I had arrived late (there is a lesson there as well). That night, I only sold one book out of the five books I had with me. The next day a friend of mine showed me a status update where someone had uploaded a statement from my speech. I paused for a minute and thought if that person had only known that I was an author with a book there, maybe I could have walked away with two sales and not just one. Now I will never know. Next time I will do two things: I will arrive early and I will be prepared to talk about my book.

Recap...

Do not miss out on a chance to share your product/service. Do not become entrapped by the net of being shy. Your job is to bring awareness to your product/service and increase the chances of a sale as you do this. Obscurity is your enemy: banish that enemy by letting people know.

So which category of the Belief Matrix© do you fall into? Which category applies to your product/service? Which applies more to your prospects? How do you plan on getting into the 2nd category?

So, what next?

Now that you know the importance of belief, let us chat about semblance – the setting for your sale.

CHAPTER 2
SEMBLANCE

Every sale is made within a setting. By setting, I mean that it is conducted in a place and with a person. If the salesperson is dressed the part, speaks the lingo of the relevant industry and picks a relevant place to conduct business, then the salesperson stands a huge chance of influencing the sale their way. If the wrong setting is chosen then the salesperson has an upward hill to climb.

Let us start with your dress code.

Dress Code...

In every industry that we engage in there is a certain lingo and dress code that is adhered to. Knowing the relevant dress code in your industry and looking the part allows you to become more persuasive. This is imperative to you succeeding.

I remember, as a financial adviser, I read a book called, *"How I went from Zero to Millions in Selling."* By Frank Bettger. There was a chapter that dealt specifically with the dress code. It emphasised how salespeople within the insurance industry should be dressed. For men, this translates to suits, ties, and well-polished shoes. For ladies, it included heels, pencil skirts and blouses. My thoughts were that women had greater flexibility in this regard and what I have listed is merely a drop in the ocean. Lastly, grooming falls within our dress code. We had to be well-groomed and tidy.

I prefer wearing shorts, slippers, and t-shirts because I visualise myself living in a house overlooking the ocean. This dress code is apt for my envisioned lifestyle. Seeing that the dream is in the making and that sales are really about the prospective client and not my needs, it is important to ensure that the dress code inspires the prospect to favour the proposal I bring to the table.

I took what Frank Bettger said in his book and compared it to another book by Robert Cialdini that speaks on influence. It has an interesting case study that spoke about how you can be 80% more persuasive by just looking the part. The adage that light travels faster than sound allows for such a huge percentage. This, however, means that we could miss out on deals simply because we do not allow ourselves to dress the part or show up as well-groomed individuals.

I encourage you to find out about the norms in your industry regarding dress code. Find out what the top earners wear when they see their prospects. Do you have the same type of wardrobe? If not, how could you get that type of clothing without incurring too many costs? If you are an entrepreneur and are about to pitch for new business, do some research on the dress code that would appeal to your investors or prospects. Also, ensure that you are well-groomed. Remember that in addition to the dress code, it is also essential to be well-groomed. There is no point in having the best threads on while looking scruffy.

How you look gives an impression to your prospect that you would be able to take care of them as a client. If you cannot dress decently or be well-groomed, then that puts into question how you would handle their business.

Being well-dressed and looking the part also gives you added confidence. This could translate in you charging more by simply dressing better. Try it!

Last story to take this point home. When I was looking for a job as a waiter during my gap year, I went handing out CVs at different restaurants near my home. A few days later, I got a call from Cappuccinos at The Grove in Pretoria. They asked that I come in for an interview. I was unconsciously dressed in black when I met with them. This is the colour that Cappuccinos' trainees wear. To cut a long story short, it was a win. I got the job because I already looked like I blended in, which was reiterated by the other waiters. Yes, I had to represent myself to the manager as well but the fact that I was dressed like one of them made it look like I was one of them.

How do the people in your industry dress?

Lingo...

In every industry, there is a lingo that is used. These are words, phrases or abbreviations and could even extend to common anecdotes. Do you know what the lingo in your industry is? Do you know what the lingo of your prospect's industry is?

When I started speaking, I learnt a few things that, when used, would show that I am very professional about what I do. For instance, using a rate card or understanding what a keynote is. Instead of using the phrase, "How many people will be at the show?" I now ask, "How many delegates will be attending the seminar?" There is a vast difference between the implications of those two questions. The former question shows that you may not be as well acquainted with the industry as you should be, whilst the latter shows that you are. The former statement may give the impression that you are a novice, the latter that you are seasoned at your craft. This could affect the possibilities of a sale. I do, however, realise that one might say that it would be dependent on your prospect and how well-versed they are with the industry lingo. That is true. Are you willing to take that chance? Knowing your lingo shows that you are prepared and professional.

If you do not know the lingo in your industry, then I suggest that you begin reading books that are relevant to your industry. There are two steps to this:

1. Read the top three books in the industry and you will have a general knowledge of the lingo used.

2. Practise the lingo by using one new word a day. This will get you used to the new words that you learn.

    In Toastmasters International they have a role at every meeting called, "The Grammarian". The Grammarian's job is to ensure proper use of the English language throughout the meeting. They also introduce a word of the day, its meaning and application. Speakers are then encouraged to incorporate that word into their speeches. This simple action allows you to do two things post the meeting: learn new words on the fly and express yourself more succinctly.

Now for the disclaimer when it comes to your new lingo. Remember the golden rule here is to be well prepared for your prospect. You want to sound like an expert in your field of endeavour but not at the expense of your prospect.

There are some people I know that have mastered four to five-syllable words in the English language. They spew these words out like they had been reading a dictionary and thesaurus throughout their childhood, if not having invented those two books themselves. When they speak, they come off as smart; but they lose the attention of the people they are speaking to because their words are not easily understood. Plus, the fact that no one walks around with a dictionary or thesaurus does not work in their favour either. Do not be like them. Do not try to talk over people and look intelligent at the expense of the prospect's attention. The proposal that you deliver has everything to do with the prospect's understanding of your proposition. If they do not understand what you are talking about; then it would harm your sale.

What would ideally work would be to use two to three-syllable words at most, while listening to gauge your prospect's use of lingo. When you get a good idea of their lingo level, ensure that you speak on their level. If you speak lower, it may come off as though you are not well-versed in that industry as mentioned before. If you speak at a level above the prospect, then you may be deemed too smart and that may intimidate your prospect. Remember that you are there to inspire them to buy your product/service. You can accomplish this simple task by listening. Listening is the key.

The last thing about the lingo: only speak about what you know. If you do not know what your prospect is talking about then perhaps changing the subject or stopping the conversation to enquire more would work in your favour. I have made the mistake of thinking I would look silly by not asking and allowing the conversation to continue. Once I remark, however, I end up looking silly. Let the false sense of pride go. Ask. If anything, it will show that you are interested.

So, what is the lingo in your industry? What books can you read that will help you with the lingo? Who can you speak to that could be of assistance?

Ambience...

The ambience is the character and atmosphere of a place. The environment in which you meet your prospect has a natural ambience to it. Why is that important? The ambience will affect how the prospect will perceive you and your product/service. You can improve your chances of influencing a sale by simply picking a place that creates an ambience that positively represents you and your product/service.

I was at a Toastmasters event when one of the speakers spoke about how a guy would ask ladies for their contact details whilst out on the street. Most of these ladies did not provide their contact details to him. He then decided that he would ask for these contact details outside a flower shop. Guess what? The number of ladies that gave him their contact details increased. Why? He chose a place that set a new ambience which inspired confidence in the ladies to engage with him.

The above example just proves that ambience matters. If it is not used to your advantage, it could harm your sales prospects.

I have some affluent friends who host their client meetings in very posh areas such as Sandton and Rosebank in Johannesburg, South Africa. I can assure you that the ambience created in those areas says something before my friends even open their mouths to speak to their prospects. As I write this paragraph, I will be meeting up with a prospect at the Michelangelo Hotel in Sandton, South Africa. He would like me to become his speech coach. Not only does this subconsciously tell me that he is serious, but it also tells me that he is willing to spend. The chances of me wanting to help him increase two-fold, not because I am chasing a sale for the fees, but because the ambience has already set the scene that money is not a thing for this gentleman. I will be well-groomed and well-dressed for this meeting. I know that may come off as wrong to some, I hear you. Remember, however, we either use these tools to our advantage or we suffer because we chose not to.

Recap...

The clothing that you wear and the ambience you set can determine an outcome before you even open your mouth. Why not use those to your advantage to ensure maximum support from your prospect? When supported with the right lingo, this will further add to the subliminal avalanche you have already launched on your prospect. Remember, you are not doing this to be unethical, you are simply taking into cognizance that which would aid you instead of it disempowering you.

Do you know the right environments that could set the ambience in your favour?

So, what next?

Let us scratch semblance off the list. Now we discuss how to grow that belief you have into confidence. The difference? Confidence is belief manifested.

CHAPTER 3
THE VALUE OF ROLE-PLAYING, AFFIRMATIONS AND VISUALISATIONS

Role-Playing...

It is my first week back from financial adviser training and I have a meeting with my manager, Jacques Jenneke. He wants to see what I have learnt and how the training went.

In that meeting, he suggests that we do some role-playing. If you have never done a role-play before then, like me, you would realise that it can be very weird. Here you are simulating what could happen in an actual sale. The reason why it was weird for me was that I had never done it before and the pressure was high. What would my manager think of me if I messed this up? What would I think if I messed this up? This also being my first job increased the load of pressure on my shoulders. Lastly, two adults playing pretend. That just feels wrong on so many levels. If you feel the same way, allow me to be honest and loving at the same time: what you have is pride. What you need to do is to let it go. Right, back to the story.

He decided that he would be a prospect interested in getting long-term life insurance and investments. We were at a restaurant of my choosing. I was to engage him, find out what his needs were and proceed to a sale. Even when I would imagine this was the case, I still did not know how to handle it because I never knew what to say to a prospect. The training I had received before seeing my manager was excellent but I did not translate what I had learnt into a conversation with a prospect. I was just trying to pass the training exams. You can imagine how I mixed up and fumbled my words. My manager, however, was cool, calm, and collected. I think he expected that.

Not having learnt from my lesson when I went to see actual prospects, guess what happened? I mixed up and fumbled my words there as well. Not all of them were as cool, calm, and collected as my manager was. Some bought my products while others walked away. Those were sales I could have made had I done more role-playing.

There is a direct correlation with the preparation done through a role-play exercise and the success that can be achieved during a real scenario. Getting feedback after the role-play also increases your chances of success. This also means that you need to know what you will say in advance and how you will identify the prospect buying signs.

Months later, we had a staff meeting with all the financial advisers of our company. The top earner of the organisation, Alan Roets, shared his secrets. He had a script that he used each time he went to see a prospect. He had mastered it verbatim. The fact that he was so high up the corporate ladder meant I certainly had something to learn from him. I had the voice, the charisma, lingo and looks. I needed a script. I needed to role-play. You also need a script. You also need to role-play.

A script will allow you the time and space to focus on the prospect and to look for signs of buying or resistance, only if you learn it verbatim though. There will be times when you can drift from it but the structure will ensure that you take your prospect from them not knowing and trusting you to them knowing and trusting you and being willing to buy your product/service. If you do not have a script, then you are merely getting into every conversation with no set structure. You are mini-mising your chances of a sale. Create a script and role play it. Get feedback from your role players and get them to help you improve your script.

In Toastmasters International, we learn how to deliver speeches. This builds confidence and greater articulation when communicating your ideas. Now, what does this do when you meet with people outside of club meetings? You learn to flow when it comes to telling people about your ideas. Toastmasters is like role-playing too. It is a training ground where one can learn in a safe environment. When one learns from the feedback given by evaluators, one can apply that to outside scenarios.

I was at my club, The Sages Toastmasters Club, delivering an assignment on interpersonal skills. The objectives of this assignment were to start a conversation with a stranger with ease and maintain it for 3 to 5 minutes in front of the whole club. My project came in three parts. The first part was to explain to the audience how to communicate with ease with a stranger, I would then demonstrate it and get some feedback from the audience and the chosen role player. I did the first part with ease because at this point, I was comfortable with speaking in front of an audience. The second part was scary for two reasons. Firstly, the role player and I could not have rehearsed what we were going to do. Everything had to be spontaneous. As I called the gentleman up to the front, I saw what I looked like when my manager asked that we do a role-play. At least Jacques did not do this to me in front of an audience. The second reason for my fear was that I not only had the responsibility of completing my task with flying colours, but I had to ensure to keep my nerves at bay by being calm so that Isaac, the role player, would be calm too.

Isaac arrived at the front of the room and we began to talk. I asked him a few questions to engage in conversation. I had given a presentation on the script, so I knew exactly how I was going to do this. Isaac, however, began to get nervous in front of everyone and froze. This was not part of the script, but I was able to improvise and ask easier questions and show him that he had nothing to be afraid of. This reminded me of Jacques' cool, calm, and collected demeanour. The conversation did ensue with awkward moments here and there but eventually, the 3 – 5 minutes were over. I then asked him to take a seat, got the audience to applaud him for his bravery and then went into the third part of the assignment: feedback from the audience.

I will not mention the good things people said because I knew those. Instead, I will mention the highlighted point of improvement. An audience member mentioned that I asked Isaac personal questions a bit too early in the conversation and should have rather kept asking general questions for some time and then transitioned slowly to the personal questions.

I had received this feedback before but had never considered it. Although I would still get an answer from whoever I was speaking to, there would be some hesitation. As all these scenarios played in my mind, the penny had finally dropped. From then on, I made a promise to never ask deep questions from the onset and to rather be patient and enjoy the small talk, even though I often get bored by it.

I know I certainly had improved from the time I role-played with my manager to the time that I did the role-play at the Toastmasters meeting. During both times, a penny dropped: with my manager, it was that I needed to be prepared with a script. At the Toastmasters event, it was to engage in small talk for longer before asking personal questions. These have certainly helped me in real-life scenarios.

The greatest sports personalities do this. They, however, call it a practice which confirms the adage, "the more you sweat in practice the less you bleed in battle." Kobe Bryant, Michael Jordan, Serena Williams and Cristiano Ronaldo, to mention a few, all do this. This allows them to ensure that while the crowd is cheering and the stakes are high that whatever they are about to do has been done before, it is just a matter of repeating it with some slight adjustments.

When your bills are high and you need to make that sale, ensure that you have a written script which you have practised and role-played. All that would be left would be to follow through with it while incorporating the feedback you would have received. You will be more confident about it.

If you want to take this further and get yourself to build more confidence, then I would suggest that you learn how to create affirmations and a vision board.

Affirmations...

Affirmations are statements or propositions declared to be true. The reason they are so popular is that when one utters affirmations to themselves, whether they are true or false, our subconscious registers them as real and we act accordingly. If someone repeats, "Money always comes to me" enough times, the subconscious mind will believe this and they will begin to see opportunities where large amounts of money could be made. This is not an overnight process. I have some affirmations that have materialised and others that are yet to. The big lesson in all of this is that you should watch the words you say. Positive statements will bring about a positive attitude that would get you to seek positive results. The converse is also true.

Before I get up to speak, whether it is at Toastmasters, church or for a professional event, I get nervous and feel a barrage of butterflies fly in my gut. Most of my friends tease me because they wonder whether nerves are even part of my vocabulary. How I ensure that these butterflies fly in a formation is that I say the following affirmation: "I speak and mountains move." I keep repeating that as I bring to remembrance how in the past people have cheered fanatically. Once I am in front of the audience, time stands still. I take a deep breath and realise it is time to move mountains. Which I always do.

You can look up positive statements that you can repeat to yourself. The most effective time to do this is when you are about to sleep or when you have just woken up. Personally, however, I do them as much as I can before I do a certain task. You could also read a book by John Kehoe called "*Mind Power.*" It would further clarify the potency of affirmations. In his program, he highlights one of my favourite affirmations which I repeat before a phone call to a prospect: "sales and success today, sales and success today."

Visualisations...

To add to the confidence that you are building, you could learn to do visualisations as well, especially after an affirmation. I always see these mountains moving and the crowd benefiting richly from my speech. I then see them happily buying a signed copy of my book as well. So, when someone says, "Great speech!" I do not act surprised; I do however say, "Thank you." Then when someone asks me, "How much is your book?" I respond with "R200, who will I be signing it to?"

Visualising helps because once you have mentally pictured it, it does not feel foreign to you. That allows you to be like Jacques: cool, calm, and collected.

Visualise the product/service that you are offering to be something that your prospects want. Picture the meetings with your prospects going well and them buying your product/service. It may not always go the way you expect it to, but the chances of a sale going through increase. I have experienced this.

Visualising goes far beyond just preparing for a sale of a product/service. You can use it for the largest sale in your life, opulence.

Kim Wetzl, a good friend of mine and successful entrepreneur, told me something interesting. When she was younger, she would play in her father's garage and visualise herself teaching students. She did this for years. Her brothers would sometimes bully her and during those times she would leave the house to go to a nearby hill and build small houses out of branches and debris that she would find. What was interesting is that when she would come back to this hill, she would find someone living in that small home. Given, it was probably not the best of places to stay in, but someone chose to stay in it.

Years later, she became the owner of a school called ABC International, a school that teaches people how to speak English. This is a useful service if you did not have English as a first language in high school. Most of her clients are foreigners who learn English to get into the local universities in South Africa. She also owns multiple properties around South Africa, including her school building.

She worked ridiculously hard to get to where she is, however, there is a testament that visualisations had an impact on her success.

Visualisations are powerful. Use them and add to your arsenal of confidence. You will have to work, however, and as you do, your visualisation will come into being.

Another form of visualisations is vision boards.

Vision Boards...

A vision board is board or piece of paper, preferably A3, depending on how large your dreams are. You take cut-outs of places you would like to see, things you would like to do, people you would like to meet, the money you would like to earn or cars and clothes you would see yourself obtaining. Whatever your dream is, you find a picture that represents it. You then take these pictures and create a collage. This is where you see all your dreams regularly. This is powerful because your subconscious mind begins to associate itself with your dreams. It then begins to look for solutions to get your current reality to that of your dreams. If you can have a picture on that poster that deals with your success with your product or service then eventually it will happen, just be patient and put in the work. To further clarify, it is not about time, it is your actions that matter. The more you act, the quicker your dreams will become a reality.

You can select what you think would work best for you. I have seen people in my circle begin to get what they visualise. I also have one and would like to share the following disclaimer with you; it works if you do too. Each day you look at it you will be reminded about what is important. What propels you forward will be the ideas that come to mind to achieve what is on the vision board. Consistently following those ideas up with vehement execution directly determines whether you will actualise your dreams or not. It only works if you do.

Recap...

Do you have a sales script? Who are you going to role-play it with? Do you have affirmations, visualisations or a vision board that will help build your confidence? The more devices you have in your arsenal of confidence, the higher your chances of success.

So, what next?

You are now developing confidence. Next, I want to take you one step back and then propel you forward like an arrow to a predestined target. Let us talk about understanding the need.

CHAPTER 4
IS THERE A NEED?

Google describes a need as a verb. It is described as requiring something because it is essential or especially important rather than just desirable.[1]

In the Sales Rings of Insight©, the next ring after belief is understanding if there is a need for what you would like to sell.

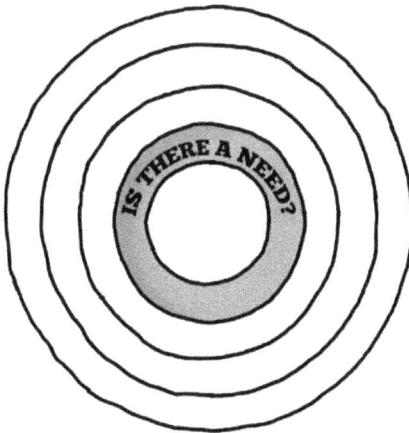

Figure 6 - Sales Wheel of Insight © - Is there a need?

---

1   https://www.google.com/search?q=need+definition&oq=need+definition&aqs=chrome..69i57j0l6.31606j1j7&sourceid=chrome&ie=UTF-8

What you are selling must satisfy a need. Whoever you are selling to must see the relevance of what you are selling and how they need to part with their money for your product/service, because of how it solves a problem for them.

There are two things you need to investigate. The first is what problem you are solving for the prospect. The second is to be able to articulate how your product/service addresses a specific need.

Needs

There is a gentleman named Abraham Maslow who created a framework in 1943. I got acquainted with this framework while studying my undergraduate degree. Maslow was able to articulate the hierarchy of needs that every human goes through and dubbed his findings the "Maslow's Hierarchy of Needs." Creative? Not really, but what is important is understanding its implication in your sales process.

Human needs are grouped into three categories:

1. Basic needs which consist of physiological needs: food, water, warmth and rest. Then your safety needs like security.
2. Psychological needs, the need to have friends and intimate relationships.
3. Self-fulfilment needs.

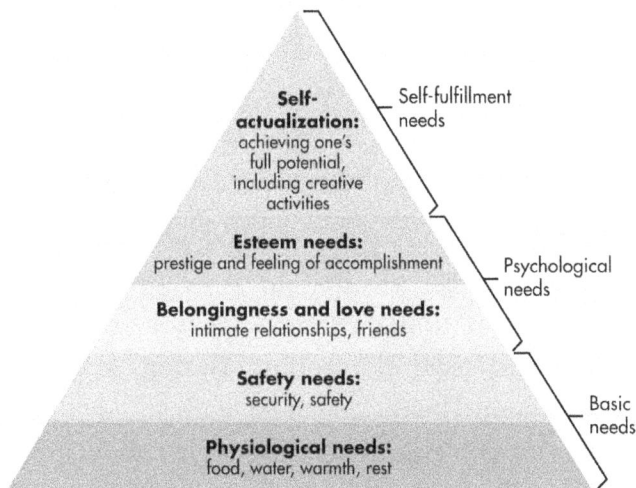

Figure 7 – Maslow's Hierarchy of Needs[2]

What need does your product/service fulfil?

Every prospect you see will be trying to fulfil one of those needs. You must be noticeably clear where your product fits in if you want to have success.

One of the services we offer is author coaching and publishing. If you have a look at the image above, that easily falls at the top of the triangle. If the prospect we see does not have a home, security, or a feeling of belonging, then to sell the service we offer to them will be null and void. They have other needs that should be addressed first.

---

2   https://www.simplypsychology.org/maslow.html

What you should also note is that the higher you go up that ladder, the less motivation you need. If my basic and psychological needs are met, then self-fulfilling needs are an option. Options can be rejected; what cannot be rejected are physiological and safety needs.

You will also see that most of the time, the higher you go up that triangle, the more expensive the product/service. Sleeping, water, food and warmth would be the cheapest, with some of those needs being for free depending on the country you reside in. Once you go one level up; you would have to pay for accommodation to keep safe. When those two basic needs are sorted you would want to be part of a community. You would have to pay for that in one way or another. Whether it is for meals, gifts for birthdays or with your most expensive commodity, time.

So, what now?

Once you know exactly what need you serve, the next step is to understand that you need to sell it like it is a basic need. That it is a must-have and not a want or desirable.

I remember selling life cover to a prospect. He saw what I was selling as a self-fulfilment need. So, the urgency to buy was not apparent. My job was simple. I had to answer the question, "How do I motivate this man to buy into the insurance I am selling?" I transitioned that conversation by reminding him that if anything were to happen to him, his family would be left in a compromising position. How would his family cope without him being able to provide for them anymore, whether disabled or if he were to die? I went straight to psychological needs and perhaps the basic need for safety too. The result? He bought life insurance from me on that day.

The same can be said about our business as publishers or author coaches. We must sell those as psychological and basic needs otherwise there is no urgency for one to buy.

Now you may be thinking, "Grant, isn't that manipulative though?" Well, that depends. If you honestly believe that what you offer is a solution to the person you are serving, then I would suggest that you ensure you leave with the sale. If on the other hand, you realise that what you are offering does not form a solution for the prospect, please have enough integrity to walk away. The point is not to meet your quota at the expense of a prospect. The point is to ensure their need is met and that they will not obstruct themselves from the solution. I will share more about that in future chapters.

Recap...

Do you know the need your product/service solves for? How can you sell it as a basic or psychological need to increase the urgency of the sale?

So, what next?

To know a need is one thing, you would still have to monetise it. Shall we chat about that next?

CHAPTER 5
CAN THE NEED BE MONETIZED?

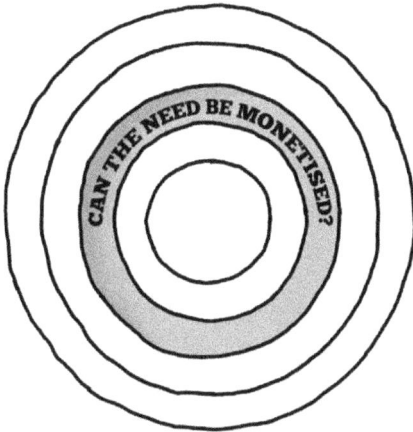

Figure 8 - Sales Wheel of Insight © -
Can the need be monetized?

This chapter is really for the entrepreneur, whether aspiring or accomplished. You need not read this if you do not own a business nor seek to own one.

Let us begin...

Whatever product/service you are selling needs to come at a price. If it does not, then you have a non-profit organisation on your hands and not a business.

Another catch ...

If you charge too little for your product/service, you not only run the risk of going broke but also looking cheap in your prospect's eyes. For some reason, we have been conditioned to think the more expensive a product is, the better the results. Charge too much and guess what? You risk not having any clients.

There are three things that I would want you to understand about your pricing structure. I learnt these three things from a discussion I had with Marco Jacobs. The three pricing structures he mentioned were that you either price at cost, on par with your industry or with a handsome amount of profit.

1. At cost of production

This is when one charges enough to cover what it took to make the product. So, if the item cost you R5 000 to make then you will charge exactly R5 000. There is nothing wrong with this way of doing business in certain scenarios. For instance; if you have a special on a specific product/service or you are a new entrant into the market and would like to get noticed. You could be looking to end a certain product line. The last scenario where this works well is when the product/service is bundled with other products/services.

2. *On par with industry prices*

The second price that people charge is what their competitors are charging. While it is important to already have known this beforehand, I feel what is equally important to know is why your competitors are charging those prices. Do not just charge for the sake of it; always find out why. This could allow you to see gaps that you would have never seen. It would also allow you to change pricing more intentionally. Also, note that competing on price is a no. In the eyes of your prospect, you want to offer a solution to their problem and offer value for doing it. Anything less will cause you to be part of the, "I am still deciding list" when you follow up with your prospect.

3. Price above industry standards

If you are charging this amount, there must be a good reason for it. One reason might be that your goods are in high demand and therefore, charging a high price would allow for a better flow of supply. The second reason is that you could be well-positioned as an expert in your field and could charge a higher rate. You could also have products/services that only serve a niche market which has a lot of money. This is where you want to be.

I would like to say that you can charge whatever you want, but that would not be good advice. I will encourage you to do your research and ensure that you are charging a price that supports your business and allows it to grow. If not, then the longevity of your business might be in question.

Negotiating...

Prospects love to negotiate, especially if you are a consultant. If you enter a shop, the price is usually what it is. You will pay the price listed on the shelf. When you are a consultant, however, people get the urge to ask for discounts and whether you can reduce your price for future business. If you are charging near your cost price, the negotiation may push you to fall below that. This could lead you to realise a loss. Not only does this hurt your business, but it is also demoralizing. The customer walks away with your product and you walk away with less than what you put in to make it. Every engagement should end in a win-win. They win by having your product and you win by charging a healthy price.

When negotiating with a client and they ask for an upfront discount, please only do so for two reasons. Firstly, if they will pay you a lump sum upfront instead of numerous payments or secondly if they will be buying some other product/service from you. If not, it will waste your time and your finances. If they mention that they will give you future business: great! Agree and mention that they will pay the full price for the first product/service and the rest will be discounted. Then get an agreement on paper. This is to ensure that there is a win-win. If they are genuine with their offer, they will agree to your terms, if not then you are in a favourable position. It may be in your best interest to walk away.

Recap...

What I am about to share with you is contrary to everything that I have said thus far and is based more on feelings than on facts. Learn to follow your gut feeling. When I published my first book, I was advised to sell my book for R150 a copy. "This works well if you are a new author." Was the advice I received. Deep inside, however, my gut kept telling me that I should certainly charge more. I thought that R200 would have been fair. I charged R160 a copy at the book launch and sold more of my copies that evening. Following that day, I charged R200 a copy and the copies are still flying. I tend to ask myself the question, "What would have happened if I had charged R200 from the onset?" I should have been confident enough to charge and stick to that. I now follow my gut feeling for my current products and services.

Charge the right price by listening to your gut feeling and understanding your market.

What price are you going to charge and why?

So, what next?

"No sales book is complete if it does not have objection handling." Anna Ngarachu, also an avid salesperson, once mentioned to me as I proposed the idea of this book. She is right. Let me share with you how to handle objections.

CHAPTER 6
OBJECTION HANDLING

Every salesperson will tell you that objection handling is a must-have in your arsenal. Whoever you are trying to transition from prospect to client will sometimes give you reasons why they do not want to buy or commit to your product/service. For the novice, objection handling is simply when your prospects give more excuses for not buying your product/service than concrete reasons.

All the sales books that I have read introduced slick ways of handling objections. While I laughed and marvelled when reading these; I would hesitate to use them. Handling objections should be rooted in looking at the client and seeing whether they are getting in their way or not. You do not have to be slick about this. You do not have to have a fancy way of dismantling an objection. My advice is that when you hear an objection from a prospect, just speak to them as you would a friend.

The reason for this is that you want them to come to a point where they make a decision that is the best fit for them. Whether that decision will benefit you or not. Therefore, it should never be about trying to get your quota up. That is manipulative and self-serving and will always come back and haunt you soon enough.

When I left my job at Liberty Life, I received a call from a company selling Wi-Fi routers. I remember telling the lady that I had no money as I had no job. She handled that objection very well and I took up the offer. Now you may say, "Grant, that's your fault, not hers." And you would be right. Ultimately, I was to blame and it was my fault because I have ultimate responsibility for my actions. Here is the thing, you can take that road too as a salesperson. You can make the argument that the customer/client should know better and how as the salesperson you are not at fault. You would be right, but there is a sense of empathy here that I believe is missing from that equation. You may have won that sale but you would have left the customer/client worse off and I don't know if that would be worth merely reaching your quota.

That being said...

Now that I have given you the disclaimer, let me share with you how to handle objections. The following section will show you the objections faced, what problem the buyer may be facing and a possible solution towards it.

Types of Objections...

They are seven objections you are likely to face:

1. Price

Problem:
1. The price is high but they can afford it.
2. The price seems to not justify the outcome they want.
3. They blatantly can't afford it.

Solution:
1. Ask what their budget is. If they do not have one, stick to your price and ask for the sale. Chances are they are just making an observation.
2. Talk about the need they wish to satisfy and how continuing with their current solution(s) might cost them more.
3. Have a price structure that is broken up into smaller payments, as this objection is usually about upfront payment. If they show that they still cannot afford it, then let it go, it is not worth it. Assure them that when they are ready, you will be too. It will leave the meeting with positive energy.

2. Complacency

Problem:

- This is when your prospect does not understand their problem and that buying your product/service will save them either time or money in the end.

Solution:

- Do your homework beforehand and know the prospect's pain in detail and how much time or money they are throwing away by not buying from you.

- If you have this information at hand, keep reminding them that their current solution isn't solving their problem. If, however, they persist in keeping their current solution; walk away.

3. Fear of change

Problem:

- No one is fond of change. Particularly the risk it may take if they were to change.

Solution:

- Usually, the problem is that the prospect needs to know they will have your support throughout the change. You could also comfort them with the fact that other people have felt the same way but felt better for making the change.

4. Trust

Problem:

- A prospect does not trust you or they do not trust your product/service. The key is to ensure that you show how other people trust either you or your product/service.

Solution:

- It is important to have accolades or awards within your industry. Prospects want to know that you will deliver. Ensure that you are dressed for the part, you use the right lingo and you have picked the right place for the meeting. As you speak to them ensure to weave in testimonials of people you have helped and awards you may have won. It will do you well in building the trust you would need.

5. Previous bad experiences

Problem:

- We have all had a bad experience with a salesperson. In light of that experience, we cringed when we had someone from that industry approach us with more or less the same product/service.

Solution:

- If they agreed to see you and have mentioned prior experiences to you, then there is an element of trust. Your work here is to show and tell them how you have treated clientele in the past. Note, I didn't say how you will treat them in the future because that already lets them know that their fear of a repeat problem may happen again. You have to show that you have a track record.

6. External input

Problem:

- I could tell you stories about this. "I would like to ask my husband/wife" or "You know other people are saying…" I have heard it all. Including "I need to pray about it."

Solution:

- When these things happen, the best thing for you to do is ask what that person would say if they were in the room with you two. Pause, and let them say what is really on their mind. 9/10 times they will tell you. If they, however, respond with, "I don't know what to think" and you have presented well. Letting it go might be your best bet.

- My experience with this type of objection is that the prospect is too afraid to let you know what may be on their mind so they use something external to make a point.

7. *Timing*

Problem:
- Sometimes it is not the right time for your prospect to buy. When this happens and you realise that this is genuine; do yourself the favour of asking when it would be a better time. Write it down then contact them at that specific time.

Solution:
- Do not lose their contact details because, from personal experience, I have realised these people are saying yes. Just not at that moment.

Now let me share how to handle objections. There are three things to do. Firstly, you need to listen to what they have to say, acknowledge it and then ask, "If we were to (drop the price, show you need the product/service, speak to other people that bought before, show our track record of superb customer service, have your external party agree, or pushed it to another time) would you be keen to purchase the product/service?" Wait for their response: it is coming. If they say yes, then think about how you can handle their objection. If they say no, you could ask why and repeat the above process unless you realise that it is not worth your while. Trust me, you will know.

Ask for the deal...

Figure 9 - Sales Wheel of Insight © -
Close: Have you asked for the sale?

Most salespeople believe that their prospects will buy after delivering a great presentation. From experience, I can tell you this much: you can deliver the best presentation, but if you do not close the sales process by asking the prospects to buy, then you are wasting your time and your prospects' too.

Over time I have realised why as salespeople we do this. Some would mask it as being afraid of rejection; I believe it is rather the fear of being vulnerable. Asking for something subconsciously gives power to the person you are asking from. We inadvertently also admit that we need someone else to make a decision.

Here is the whole truth, however, asking for the sale allows for both yourself and the prospect(s) to engage in a choice together. You are almost saying, "I think you would be better off with this and here are the reasons why." Then you would close with "If you agree, will you buy?" which is followed by a silence that could either lead to acceptance or rejection.

While you may think it is better to skip through this, you may forget the most important point. This sale needs to be part of their journey as much as it is yours. You need to allow them to come to the party with you. Not everyone will say yes to you and that is fine. Remember your job is to bring a solution to someone who needs it. This means that you will go looking until you find them and every "no" that comes your way increases the probability of you finally getting to the "yes" you seek.

So ask and keep asking. Be vulnerable enough to get to your "yes". From experience, I can tell you this much. Your yes is waiting for you, but will only expose itself when you do. Ask.

Recap...

I will say it once more, objection handling is best used for interested prospects that are setting up excuses to prevent them from a better life through your product/service offering. Trying this with people who couldn't care less will waste your time and effort. The interesting thing is that your intuition will tell you when you meet either of those two individuals. Will you listen when it speaks? That is the question.

Lastly, remember to ask for the sale. The sales process is not complete unless you ask. Let go of the fear of being vulnerable and embrace the fact that your yes can only appear when you become vulnerable enough to ask for it.

So, what next?

How about we talk about numbers? Not profit or loss orientated but rather around productivity.

CHAPTER 7
NUMBERS DON'T LIE

"Numbers do not lie" is a wise statement that Jay-Z, a highly acclaimed musician, mogul, and businessman mentioned in one of his songs. The statement he used has a trove filled with gems. Take time to think it through. These are some numbers that would be relevant to you:

1. The amount of money in your bank account.
2. The amount of money in your wallet.
3. The amount of money you receive as a salary.
4. The number of friends you have.
5. The litres of fuel in your car.
6. The amount of clothing you own.
7. The amount of time you have been with your spouse.
8. Your current age.
9. The number of qualifications you have.
10. The number of siblings you have.

All the above are numbers and they all give us an idea of who you are. They may not be accurate, but they do give us a general idea. You can tell me that you are rich, but once I investigate your bank account, I will know how truthful your statement is. You can tell me your business is doing well, but I will only be certain once I see your financials.

I once stumbled upon an opportunity from a friend. His family was selling their liquor store. I am always up for new opportunities. This time around, however, I was more intelligent than when my brother and I had got into the vending machine business a few years ago. We bought units simply on the premise that they would produce a great income, especially when we considered the vending machine salesman's advice. The salesman gave us numbers and we did not question them. We just bought into it and we paid a hefty price for our ignorance.

Determined to not make the same mistakes; I asked my friend for a meeting to view the liquor store. I also asked for financials. This would equip me to ask relevant questions about this potential investment before requesting financial assistance to acquire it.

Numbers allow you to have an incorruptible idea of where you are. They show progress or highlight improvement areas. As you learn how to sell, you will also have to learn how to record certain metrics. Recording these metrics allows you to improve your sales process by revealing possible pitfalls and the advantages you are making the most of.

I hated this process due to its administrative burden. I just wanted to do stuff and have fun while doing it. If this is you, then you have two alternatives. You could either hire someone who will handle your administration, or you could begin to learn for yourself. I would advise the latter. The reason for this will surface later.

The numbers I was looking for were the business' financials. I wanted a statement of income, a balance sheet, and a cash flow statement. Without these financial documents, I could not make any decisions. After several attempts to get these documents, I got the response that they were not willing to provide these to me. The result? The deal between them and me fell through. Interestingly, when the business owners had bought into the business, they also did not ask for the financial documents. It makes sense why they were not doing well and were probably hesitant in showing me those documents.

Whilst working as a financial advisor, I was asked to record the number of phone calls I would make, then how many of those phone calls turned into meetings, then how many meetings turned into second meetings and what the prospects bought during those second meetings.

Was this a tiresome and gruelling process? Yes! However, when I finally got into the swing of things, guess what? It all began to make a lot of sense. From the recording, I was able to derive ratios. I knew that if I called ten people, I would be able to get at least six appointments depending on the relationship I had with the person or if they were referred to me. If they were a cold lead, I would make one appointment out of ten calls. Already these numbers tell me that I had a higher influence on referrals and people I knew. Out of those six people that I would have appointments with, four of them would ask me to generate a quote. Three out of the four would then buy.

Therefore, if I wanted to increase the number of people that bought into my product, guess what I needed to do? I could increase the number of people I called, which means if I increased it to twenty calls, I would then be able to double the other numbers as well. It would then increase my sales from three to six. I could also keep the number of calls the same and instead decide to rather look at the script I use when I call these people. If I increased that to eight appointments, because of a better script, then I could increase the number of second appointments and thus increase my sales by 20%.

The last consideration was increasing the number of calls to twenty instead of ten and improving my sales script. It would mean 16 more appointments which lead to ten possible follow up sessions with quotes and therefore seven to eight people buying my services.

This is the power of recording your sales activities. As you would have noticed though, it is not only about recording but finding out the reason behind the ratios.

The truth behind ratios...

I would recommend that you record your activities for at least two sales cycles. From the first call made to the sale. The reason for the recommendation is because the first cycle requires just recording while the second cycle removes outliers.

Break down all the ratios and then ask yourself these questions:
1. Did I have the correct script?
2. What was I wearing?
3. Where did I meet them?
4. Was I organised when I met them?

There are many other questions you could ask, the more questions the better but only if it brings more clarity which makes you act.

For this book, I decided that to record the number of words I typed within ten minutes consistently. I watched these numbers closely. When I started, I produced about 300 words per 10 minutes. This meant that I could produce 1800 words within an hour.

I then added music when I typed and ensured that I had a general idea of what I wanted to type. I also needed to ensure that no one would disturb me, so I woke up much earlier when I knew that everyone in my home would be asleep. I know with most experiments you are meant to change one thing at a time to see what makes a difference. If you have the time, I would advise the same. If you are like me, however, and do not have the time, then I think changing multiple things at the same time would help. The result of my changes equated to 400 words per 10 minutes.

What is the relevance of all of this? You see, my books average a word count of 20 000 words which means that if I decided to write a full unedited manuscript then all I needed to do was work out my current stats to figure out how long it would take me to get there. If I wake up early consistently, play music on repeat and have a general plan for what I am going to write about then I should get to 20 000 words in (400*6 = 2400 words per hour, 20 000/2400 = 8.4) 8-9 days.

Is that impressive? I certainly think so! It becomes more impressive when I compare the fact that it took me two years to write my first book, which was much shorter than this book. If 8-9 days will bring too much strain then, I could decide to rather write for 30 minutes a day. This just means that my manuscript would be done in 16 – 18 days. I can continue to manipulate these numbers until I get the outcome that works for me.

This is the value of knowing your numbers and reviewing them to find ways to surpass them. If you look up any pro-athlete or someone who is the master of their craft, then you would notice that they all have a number that they work with, too.

Even entrepreneurs know their numbers...

Mark Chivere, chief executive of Accelerate Performance, and Nicole Larissa, founder and CEO of Coco, always record their activities. They have both mentioned how that helps with making important decisions in their respective companies. These decisions range from whether to improve a certain product/service or to discontinue it. Their numbers give them clarity and cut out all ambiguity.

Mark's key metric to review was the time of the month that a consultant would purchase personality tests from him. He often mentioned that those who purchased their tests in advance and on the 1st of the month were usually more successful than those that waited for the demand of the personality test before requesting them from him. Naturally, his priority went to the consultants that purchased in advance and on the 1st of every month. Their success ultimately led to his business' success.

Had Mark not paid close attention to such detail, guess what may have been the outcome? It would have been wasted time, which would have resulted in poor company growth.

For her business, Nicole would review the time it took to make a product and whether it was worth selling once all the costs were summed up. This knowledge allowed her to decide on the product/service to discontinue or to continue with.

Recap...

Have you set up a system to help you record the numbers? What do your numbers tell you? Have you tried tweaking them? How did that change the result?

So, what next?

You have the system. Have you decided on what you will be selling and how to articulate it?

CHAPTER 8
WHAT ARE YOU SELLING?

What exactly are you selling?

Most people never really get to the crux of what they sell. They dibble and dabble at the surface and think that would be enough, but it is not.

I write books and create pragmatic keynote presentations. If I were to end my sentence there, then I too would be dibbling and dabbling because anyone can do that. What I sell is not my product/ service. It is much larger than that. It is much deeper than that too. When you cannot convey the depth of what you sell, then you become a commodity. You are then forced to compete on price which results in your product/service falling into an extremely competitive world.

To find out what you truly sell, you could work backwards. I mentioned that I sell books and develop keynotes.

Let us look at books.

Why do I write books? Why books and not magazines or any other literary work? The answer is simple: books give an authority that I would not have had had I just decided to pursue the other literary works. I was once asked whether I would ever consider that I may have just become an author for the sake of the title. On the surface, the answer is yes, with a deeper analysis I figured out that articles soon get lost, but books remain on shelves. I would like to remain on my customers' shelves.

I want to accomplish these three things in every book I write:

1. I want to enlighten my clients, whether company or individual, with a pragmatic process to help them become a better version of themselves.
2. I want to equip them with a process to use and adapt to suit their needs.
3. Lastly, I want to empower them to be able to start that process.

I do not write because of the authority that it may bring; rather I write because I want my readership to have tools and processes that will help them grow pragmatically.

So, what do I sell? I sell processes that enlighten, equip, and empower. I use my books as products to express this.

When someone now asks me, what is your book about? Or what will your keynote do for our organisation? My answer remains the same: my books and keynotes are about enlightening, equipping, and empowering you with pragmatic processes and tools that will get you to grow sustainably and then exponentially. This answer also ensures that I could change the product/service that I offer, by expressing it differently perhaps through a workshop, seminar, or webinar. Do not get caught up in how you express what you sell, rather pay attention to what you are expressing. This would differentiate you from everyone else who would just be trying to sell a commodity.

To further differentiate myself, I would then ask myself the question, why. Why do I want to enlighten, equip, and empower people or companies with pragmatic processes and tools that will get them to grow sustainably and then exponentially?

There is a bible verse that intrigues me. Hosea 4:6 which states, "My people are destroyed because of lack of knowledge..." I know in this specific verse the context is spiritual. In Proverbs 10:14 it states, "Wise people store up knowledge, but the mouth of the foolish is near destruction." Both verses depict the importance of knowledge and that without it, death is imminent. This could be spiritual, mental, financial, emotional or within relationships. What separates us from death in any of those aspects are two things:

1. Knowledge.
2. Competence to act on knowledge.

To change anything in your life, you need the correct knowledge which needs to be acted upon with competence. Competence is the ability to do so. Therefore, the distance between you and change is what you know and the execution of that knowledge.

Where I would have stated that I sell processes that enlighten, equip, and empower. I use my books as a product to express this, and the service is pragmatic keynote presentations, on a whole deeper level. Really what I am selling is pragmatic knowledge. Put more eloquently I would say, "I eradicate death and darkness that emanates from ignorance with growth and light that emanates from practical knowledge. I do this by enlightening, equipping and empowering individuals and companies with pragmatic processes that lead to stability and exponential growth." Now I have my why. That being said; it would not be wise to say all of this to a prospect. This is for you to know and memorise and fit within a conversation more simply. In my case, it is as simple as saying "You know what TED talks do? I do that through books and speaking."

Simon Sinek argues that this is what differentiates leading companies from all others. It is not about the product; it is about why you do what you do. People and companies would buy into that much more. I would add to Sinek's argument that this is also what differentiates great people from ordinary people. Great people are propelled through the power of their why.

Finding my why and how took me some time. It has been at least five years and it changes when I realise better ways of expressing myself. I am not asking you to start with a philosophical why and how. Rather, I want you to ask yourself those questions and start with a simple statement. From that statement keep delving deeper until you get to an answer that you are happy with.

When you have your why and how the next question to ask is: who are you selling to?

Your Target Audience...

Jacques Janneke would always tell me not to knit-pick clients as it was not my job to choose which clients to sell to. My job was just to sell. This advice was given to me at the beginning of my journey of selling insurance and investment products. Upon executing his advice, he and I would sit down for our monthly one-on-one sessions, where we would then look at all the people, I sold to so we could look for patterns. Here is the point, only after I had sold my products/ services did I begin to look at who was buying. It is not something I did before, because I did not know who I appealed to. If you have records, then you can review these to identify patterns.

My patterns revealed that women bought more from me than men did. It also revealed that they were likely to buy a retirement product and then a unit trust. This made me realise that if I were in front of a lady, I would have a higher chance of making a sale and this would most likely be a retirement annuity and unit trust. I would ask why they bought from me, but that may lead me to vain assumptions. The second thing this revealed was that men were not buying my product and the question was: why? I did not know it then, but it was due to my aura. When I engage in a male-to-male conversation, I tend to become all alpha which is not a desired trait in sales. When I was with ladies, however, my more gentleman side would emerge.

I have applied my manager's advice in other facets, such as my books and our publishing services. Keep selling to those that give you the money and then look back and question the numbers.

I have heard people asking outright, "What is your target audience?" For people just entering the sales world, I would say tell them, "Right now, anyone willing to buy my product/service." Do not fall into the trap of assuming you know. You only really know when you have numbers in front of you. Even then, your numbers speak about the past and not the future. Asking yourself the relevant questions enables you to get into different market segments.

If you are still adamant about who your target market would be before sales, then looking at your why may shed some light. In my case, because I want growth and aim at it unapologetically, like-minded people would likely buy from me. My highest book sales have come from Toastmasters International members. They love growth and so do I, so they would easily buy my book. Your target audience is made up of people who believe in what you believe in. The numbers then add gender, age, race, education level, income, and profession. You have an idea of the audience you have beforehand, the specifics will come once you have sold your product/service.

The other side of the coin is that you will begin selling to those that are within your current sphere. Mum, dad, siblings, and friends. As you begin to sell more, you begin to pick up patterns on who makes up your target market. Until then though, your job is to sell.

Perhaps one last point before I conclude. I have often observed that individuals starting their sales journey would want to have a target audience. I have never seen them asking the question, however, "Do these people want to even buy from me?" Essentially, to get to the target audience you want, you need to have certain traits and mannerisms. These are built through selling to those in your closest circles as you begin to move closer to your target market.

Recap...

1. What product/service are you selling?
2. Why do you sell it?
3. How do you sell it?
4. Who do you sell it to?

So, what next?

You can now articulate what you are selling and understand why you do. Let us now discuss the importance of having a sample.

CHAPTER 9
DO YOU HAVE A SAMPLE?

In South Africa, one of the ordeals you go through when entering a mall is the bombardment of individuals trying to sell cosmetics to you.

I must admit that I am covertly impressed by these people and their courage. There is a lesson I learnt from them. Most of these sales individuals sell expensive products that you would be reluctant to purchase on the spot. They have noticed this and have, therefore, offered a sample. What does a sample do for you? It ensures that what you are buying has no risks attached to it. When money is about to be spent, especially large amounts, we look at those items and think of all the risks attached. When you have tried out a sample, however, those risks begin to diminish. The objective of a sample is to diminish the risks perceived by prospects. The other thing to take note of is that people trust what they can use. There is a disclaimer though. They can have a sample but not the full experience. Be sure to leave some room for curiosity and intrigue. This would increase the chances of a prospect paying for the full product/service.

When I was completing a speech assignment at KPMG Toastmasters on how to persuade, I delivered a demonstration presentation in which I was selling a product. After the demonstration, I asked the audience for some feedback.

The scenario was that I was selling my book, *When the Golden Goose Doesn't Lay Eggs: Lessons on Fulfilling Your Potential,* to a huge school which had made a sizeable order. I told the school principal that they could have my book as a sample. In my mind, I thought that doing so would allow for maximum buy-in. The audience, however, had a different view. They mentioned that I should have just given the principal a chapter or two; just enough to whet their appetite and then make good on closing the deal.

If you look at major outlets, like Amazon, for instance; they allow you to take a sample and let you read some of the pages within the book for free. They give the juicier portions of the book to get you interested. Stores that sell fragrances do the same thing. They do not give you a full bottle, but you are permitted to spray a bit. These are all tactics to ensure your buy-in by lowering your perceived risks of buying the item. Motivational speaker, Eric Thomas, has made a success of himself by delivering free motivational videos on YouTube. In those videos, he informs the viewers on how to get in contact with his team. If you like what you see and have a feeling that he would be the right speaker or consultant for you, then Eric has a prospect that turns into a client.

Do you have samples of your product/service that you can share?

I know this may be tougher to implement for a service as it is intangible. Perhaps, having previous customers provide testimonials or current clients endorsing you would work in your favour. Prospects want to see that the solution you offer will solve their problem. They also want to see someone whose problem you have solved and how choosing you was the best choice for the buyer at the time of purchase.

This idea also works if you know someone famous or popular. If a famous or popular person endorses you, then you are likely to receive less resistance from prospects, provided that the prospect knows that person. This association provides social proof for you. Big brands use this tactic – Nike has Ronaldo and Adidas has Missy Elliot, to name a few. People of influence are worth getting to know. It will take long for you to get there, but with time and effort, it would certainly be worth your while. In the meantime, try to get as many endorsements and testimonials as possible.

Another twist in getting endorsed by someone famous or popular is to become that person yourself. Yes, you. I have seen a lot of people trying to reach out to popular figures when sometimes the best strategy for them would have been to become that figure. This will take time, but it does put you in the driver's seat of your sales process. One of the ways I have done this is by having an online presence. I have realised over time that some prospects tend to Google you. Why not leave them with something to admire that will build your credibility? This is also a form of sampling.

Does sampling your product/service always work? No, not always. Sometimes you could lose a sale through people who merely want something for free. I remember when I was much younger, I would go into stores that have great fragrances and spray them on myself and leave. I am not saying everyone else is like that, but I am sure people have done this before. These things happen and ultimately, it is about getting your name out there and establishing some presence. These same people that get freebies may carry you through word of mouth to someone who will buy your product/service.

Sometimes, however, you would have to give a full product/service to a prospect. Be willing to, but be discerning as well. If this person is a decision-maker then perhaps getting them on your side could be advantageous. Especially if you sell it right. I will tell you of a time this worked and when it did not.

In October 2017, I had a meeting at Kingsmead College in Rosebank. Kingsmead hosts a massive book festival every year. To be considered, I was asked to bring my book along, despite having sent them a soft copy via email weeks before that. I was met by a delightful lady. She read the full book and a few weeks later, I received an email informing me that I would be one of the selected authors that would be presenting on the ideas covered in my book. This was a great achievement as I would always be known as a participant of the 2018 Kingsmead Book Festival. In this instance, having a full product worked to my advantage.

There was an incident, however, where it did not work out the way I had expected. There was a speaking engagement that I had been made aware of by my brother, Aubrey. This engagement would have 29 entrepreneurs in attendance which included insurance and investment firms. Seeing that Aubrey was going to represent us, I decided that he should have a signed copy of my book carefully wrapped in a gift bag and give this to a decision-maker. He presented the book to a decision-maker who was impressed with the gift. Her impression, however, did not turn into a sale. Therefore, things did not work out as I would have expected. What did, however, work in my stead was that she had my book and you never know when that would come in handy.

Jim Rohn gave the anecdote that seeing people and creating meetings with influencers you would like to sell to is likened to the parable of the sower. Not all your sales pitches or samples, in this case, will reap the rewards you are looking for. Over time, however, you never know who your product will land up with and how that would affect your business in the future. Keep on sowing and let the outcome handle itself.

Here is some homework.

Figure out how you can cost-effectively sample your service or product. If you can have some testimonials, it will aid the process of ensuring the risk faced by the buyer is reduced.

A little more about testimonials. The best salespeople will always be your customers. If you want to do well, give your customers mind-blowing experiences. They will sell for you from that point onwards. I have had situations where someone would be hesitant about buying my book, but once a previous customer encourages them to get the book, they are more willing to do so. Ensure that you deliver well to your customer base so that they are willing to provide testimonials.

Lastly, learn how to speak in public. Why? The fact that you are in front of an audience serves as social proof. People have entrusted you to speak to them and this intrinsically makes you seem important. Not only does it give you social proofing, but it also allows for multiple meetings to happen in one place. When you present to a large audience, you are having a personal meeting with all the delegates attending. If you do a great job with your presentation and provide details of where people can get your products and services then you could a have a large number of individuals coming to you as opposed to you visiting one person at a time. Every salesperson needs to learn how to speak in front of a large group of people. Perhaps look at the conventions that your target market would likely attend and figure out how to become a speaker on those programs. Go on, get your name out there.

Social Proofing

I realise that I have repeatedly mentioned social proofing but have not explicitly explained the term to you.

'Social proofing' is a term coined by Robert Cialdini in his book *"Influence"*. The term illustrates how people follow decisions made by large masses. It's the "95% choose this meal". It is like when a set of people are laughing and you join in even when you don't know why. It's the reason why highly rated products/services continue to sell profusely.

Social proofing allows us to limit the time taken to make a decision based on the assumption that if a lot of people bought this product/service, then it must be a good product/service. One of our needs is to fit in. If everybody is doing something, whether right or wrong, people would likely follow what has been done due to the fear of not belonging.

The point is not to determine whether this is a good or bad habit. The point is that it exists, and most people who want success in sales use it to gain an upper hand on their competition.

Recap...

Do you have a sample of your product or service? Can you find ways of getting yourself to speak to a large audience? How will you use the tool of social proofing in your favour?

So, what next?

You are making some strides. Let's discuss something you need to have to begin with. People!

CHAPTER 10
DO YOU HAVE A LIST?

Everything we have spoken about so far is important. This chapter, however, marks the hallmark of what is imperative for you to have before you even begin to sell.

You need a list.

When we teach aspiring authors on how to market their books, we ask them to populate a spreadsheet with 300 names. While you may think that this is a tough task; it is much simpler than you think.

If you have WhatsApp on your phone, this task requires that you list the names and numbers of people you regularly engage with and those you may not have spoken to in a while. If you do not have WhatsApp, it is a matter of looking at your emails (personal) or your phone book. In both situations, you start with the people you have kept in contact with then move on those you may have lost touch with.

The first 100 names are people likely to buy from you because of your strong relationship. The next 100 would just need convincing on the product, but may also buy from you because of the relationship. The last 100 would need to know why they should buy what you have and why it should be from you.

The first 100 are hot leads, the second are warm leads and the last are cold leads.

These different individuals would be engaged through your marketing message. This message is as simple as stating what problem you are solving, why your solution works and testimonials of individuals who have tried it.

You may say to yourself, "Grant, I don't have anyone that has tried my product or service yet." My response to you is to find a group of ten individuals who could try your product/service for free in return for their feedback and testimonial. This is vital for three reasons.

1) Feedback is the breakfast of champions. Whatever feedback you receive will help you to enhance your product/service. A common mistake would be providing your products/services as a gift instead of asking for feedback. Do not fall into this trap as you now know better. Get that feedback.

2) Feedback allows you to speak the buyer's language. As salespeople, we often speak

from our point of view in hopes that the person we are speaking to understands and resonates with us. However, the buyer has their language. Until you understand why they are buying in the first place, there will always be a communication breakdown. Therefore, it is imperative to get that initial feedback. Hear what your testing group likes and what problem your product/ service solves for them. Use those words when you reach out to the people on your list and your product/service will do better. The charm is in knowing that it is about the buyer and not about you.

3) Testimonials sell faster and better than you ever will. As sales individuals, we will know the problem which our product/service solves for and sell it on that basis. While this may work in the beginning; using people's testimonials will ultimately work better for you. A testimonial will tell a prospect that there are people like them who have bought the product and are happy with it. This lowers the risk they perceive and heightens the chance of them buying.

How has this worked out for me? Very well. Whenever we run the author coaching and publishing workshops, I have heard people respond with, "Oh, and they have a book now?" to which I would answer, "Yes, so when would you like to start with yours?"

The List Beyond the List

The list that I have mentioned above is your starting point. You would have to consistently add to that list regularly (weekly) so that you always have someone to see.

This means getting out of your comfort zone and networking. The equation is simple. The more people that know you, the more people you can sell to and be of assistance to. We will speak more on that towards the end of this book.

For now, I just want you to know that the list you start with must be added to. If not, you will run out of leads and your sales will stop. This has happened to me a few times. While I would love to blame the quality of the list I had, the truth is that I had not gone out to create new relationships.

If this idea scares you, then I am doing my job. Be comforted by the fact that the world will be a better place with your product/service in their hands. So, go out there and get yourself known.

Have you written your list yet? If so, how do you plan on growing it?

BEFORE THE SALE
CONCLUSION

Everything that we have covered thus far dealt with how important it is to be prepared for the sale – the first meeting with a prospect. Being prepared would allow you to have greater buy-in which would aid you in the process of persuading your prospect to buy your product/service. Preparation will allow you to be experienced as a professional and not a novice.

If you, however, are not prepared for the opportunity then it will elude you. You will be like the guy who wants to carry water back to his village with a bucket that has a hole in it. While you may gain some initial distance from the body of water you took from the river, the water will not reach its preferred destination. You would have wasted your resources: the energy it took to get you to the body of water initially and the amount of effort it took to hold what started as a heavy bucket. While you could recoup the energy you lost; time, on the other hand, would be lost forever.

Come to the river of opportunity with a bucket that has no holes in it. Diligently inspect it before you start your journey to the river.

Lastly, remember your sales are only as good as the list that you have, so make one and keep growing it.

The second part of this book deals with what to do during a sale. This is the moment when you finally meet with your desired prospect. What do you say? How do you conduct yourself? Answers to these questions lay in wait for you.

DURING
THE SALE

You have finally developed a script. This is the script that you are using to call every one of your prospects hoping to get a meeting to showcase your product/service. I know you are recording your ratios so you should know how many calls it takes to get a meeting. After a lot of persistence, rejections, and sacrifice, you finally have at least one person that says yes to see you.

You are excited and ready to wow them. You dress the part, you speak the right lingo, you are either meeting them at their place of work or a place that has the right ambience to work for you. You know exactly what you are selling and have a sample to increase the chances of their buy-in. You also know what questions to ask to both qualify the prospect and move them from prospect to client or customer. Lastly, you have done some role-playing, developed an affirmation and visualised success around this meeting.

The question now is: what else do you need to know to edge yourself closer to a deal when you are with the decision-maker? I will be dealing with this in detail within this part of the book. When you are done with this section you will be able to do the following:

1. Establish a connection.
2. Establish trust.
3. Learn how to monetise the need.
4. Learn how to persuade a large audience.

Each of these will help you along in your sales meeting(s).

Let us begin.

CHAPTER 11
OEL NGATI KAMEIE

There was a senior lady at my first sales job that I took a liking to. She was my manager Jacques' personal assistant. I would ask her from time to time "What would it take to become a successful person in this industry?" Her response was, "You have to see the people." She would then take a deep breath and in a serious tone say: "STP Mr Senzani, STP. See the people, see the people, see the people!" When you want to generate sales, it is important to see people. The more people you can see to pitch to the higher the chances of a sale.

For non-Avatar fans, if you exist. The title of this chapter is from a language in the movie, Avatar, and it means "I see you."

This lays the groundwork for your meeting and the other facet of seeing someone. It is not just about showing up to a meeting, it is about being present in that meeting as well. You are not merely seeing them as a prospect. You are seeing them as something beyond that. You are there to see their views, understand their problems and provide solutions once you have fully grasped their problems.

Within those sales meetings, you are the leader. You lead and carefully guide this prospect from pain to relief. To do so, you will have to look at three things: listening, body language and writing things down.

1) Listen

In Toastmasters International we have three pillars – prepared speaking, Table Topics (unprepared speaking) and evaluations. I will focus on evaluations for now. Speakers deliver speeches in the first segment of the program and these are evaluated against certain objectives. This may sound extremely easy because all you are doing is listening. While the rest of the audience is there to listen and be entertained, you, as the evaluator, are focusing on whether the speaker is fulfilling their objectives. You are looking out for things that they are doing well and things that they could improve on. This requires a whole new set of listening muscles.

This is the same way you ought to engage when you are listening to your prospect. While other salespeople may just be waiting for keywords to get prospects to buy their product/service; you will be different. You will be listening to the heartbeat of the problem. Ultimately, this means that you are listening with the intent of finding out how you can truly help the person in front of you. Even if the solution is not what you are offering.

This type of intentional listening will benefit you in two ways. You will be able to ask relevant follow-up questions and express your product/ services as your prospects understand them.

a) Questions

When selling your product/service, it is important to ask relevant questions. The objective of all of your questions should be to take a customer from understanding their problem to understanding how your solution will benefit them and the steps they would need to take to ensure this process is smooth and effective.

The collective title for these types of questions is discovery questions.

In the training I attended during my first job, we were taught that there are four types of questions. I will briefly describe them to you:

1) **Permission Questions**: these allow you to ask personal questions. When you are polite enough to ask these questions, it allows the

prospect to see you as empathetic and non-intrusive. During my coaching sessions, I always ask, "May I be honest with you?" that is a permission question. In the world of sales, a typical permission question would be, "To be of best service to you ma'am/sir I would need some information, may I enquire a few things from you?" Always lead with these questions. Always. They build rapport. When you do not lead with these questions and you are about to close the sale; the prospect might feel as though they have been vulnerable with you and you are using that against them. I have been guilty of doing this, which is why I am telling you this. I have also been a victim of this, which is also why I am telling you this. Cover your bases and get permission.

2) **Fact-finding Questions**: these are targeted for a specific objective. "How much do you earn?" "Where do you live?" are typical fact-finding questions. To get maximum buy-in from your prospect; you may want to start with permission questions first before you ask fact-finding questions. These questions are also there to qualify the prospect as a potential buyer, so not asking these questions will turn a sales

appointment into a waste of time. Qualify the prospect, ensure that the meeting is worth both of your time.

3) **Feeling-finding Questions**: these are targeted for subjective information. "How do you feel about retiring rich?" or "On the scale of 1 to 10 how would you feel if...?" The point of these questions is to find out how much of a pain your prospect is in and how soon they would want a solution to their pain. Understanding this would also allow for these questions to form the basis for the solution you provide. Remember, people buy because of emotions and they justify them with facts. You obtain these emotions through the feeling-finding questions. Including a mix of fact-finding and feeling-finding questions will get you closer to success than using just one of these.

4) **Follow-up Questions:** these would be things that may not be clear to you as your prospect answers the above three questions. A good follow up question would either fall into the fact-finding or feeling-finding questions and would be based on the information you have gathered from your prospect.

Now to simplify the three points I have just shared with you; I have created the Questions Loop© below. The loop illustrates how you should start with permission questions, proceed to fact-finding questions and then feeling-finding questions. Remember that this is a continuous loop. While you may not always ask permission questions, remember to go from fact-finding to feeling-finding questions.

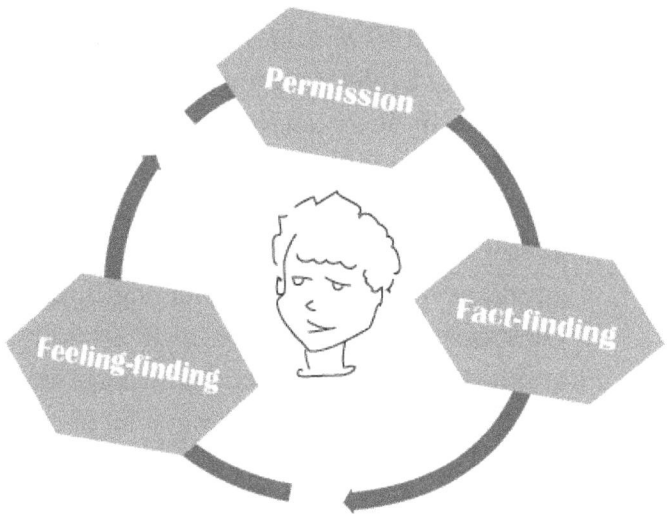

Figure 10 – The Questions Loop ©

b) Rhetoric

The second benefit of listening intently is that it allows us to also use the prospect's rhetoric. Humans are naturally vain (I mean that most respectably). If someone sounds like you, you are more likely to listen to them. Take for instance the ways we describe things that are unique to us. I am also sure you know that person whose accent changes depending on who they are talking to. I used to judge people that would do this until I realised that it was their way of saying, "Hey, I would like to communicate with you. Not to fit in but to understand and be understood." This is amazingly effective.

As you listen to your prospect, learn how they communicate. Are there any words that they keep using? If so, then communicate to them by using those words and how they describe things. If you can notice these, it would be great to reiterate those words often, whilst remaining yourself. For instance, "Ma'am you mentioned how you would want this event to put you on *the map*. In what ways have you done this before and how would you want things to be different this time around?" If "the map" is the phrase they used, then you would be communicating at their level. When using this technique, it is important to ask your prospect what they mean by certain words. That way when you use them in conversation, you both are on the same page.

How would you use your solution in a sentence for a close? I am glad you asked that fact-finding question. You would say something on the lines of,

"Well ma'am/sir I could put you on *the map* in several ways. I see in the past you may have done X, Y and Z which got you the current results. We could do A, B and C. On a scale of 1 – 10, how do you feel those solutions would help put you on *the map*?" Pause and do not say a word until they do. No matter how awkward it feels to you. The prospect is thinking and will get back to you. If you speak before they do, guess what will happen? An objection like, "Hmmm, let me think about it." will rear its head. Relax, keep calm, and listen for their response.

Let us now chat about body language.

2) Body Language

My experience is birthed from trying this out in the field and sharpening my knowledge by reading body language and a few pick-up artist books.

There is a phenomenon called mirroring. The next time you enter a coffee shop, have a look at the people sitting in pairs or groups. Look for similarities in their body language. Do they all cross their arms? Are they smiling at each other continuously? Are their legs crossed or are they all tapping their feet in mid-air? If you can see it, either in the coffee shop or in your mind's eye, then what you are witnessing is called mirroring. When we agree with something or are congruent with the person we are speaking to, we begin to mirror them. They smile, we smile. They laugh, we laugh. They cry… well you get the point. The converse is also true; when we do not agree with them, our body language shows it. They smile, we fret. They laugh, we keep a straight face. They cry… I will let you complete that one in your mind.

You may want to mirror your prospect – I don't mean fully acting like them. Just look for simple gestures that are positive. If this person crosses either their arms or legs, do not mirror them. If they frown or fret, do not mirror them if it has to do with your product/service.

The only time I would ever advise someone to mirror negative body language is if you asked the prospect what the matter was and you have the solution to that problem. If you have the solution, briefly mimic them, but as you share the solution begin to change your negative body language into positive body language. If your prospect agrees with you, they will mirror you. If not, keep asking fact-finding questions. The reason I mention fact-finding as opposed to feeling-finding is that you need to deal with their logic and not feelings. Logic stemming from the answers to fact-finding questions can be challenged and articulated.

Manipulative much?

You are not doing all of this to lead your prospect into making a decision that is not in their favour. You are doing this to ensure that you break through any barricades that may stop them from taking a solution that would benefit them. We all get like this. We know we should go to the gym, but once it is time to go and complete our sets, we find ways to get out of it.

The scenarios on mirroring covers situations where you and the prospect are seated. The rule of thumb is that deals are made when you are seated and not when you are standing. If the prospect stands while you are still doing the deal then do not get up. Remain seated until you both have concluded. Trust me, this works. The first time I heard of this concept was from Grant Cardone. I thought, "What a bunch of hogwash!" Until I saw this in action. I had to convince a business owner about my services and when I showed them the amount, this person got out of their seat and walked around frantically. I remained calm, still and smiling. After their frantic walk, they sat down with me and we engaged once more. After some discussing and negotiating, I left that room with a signed contract.

All salespeople are leaders because they take someone from where they are to a place where they are better off. Once you view the time spent with your prospect in this light, you will be able to increase your sales numbers.

Now let us talk to the third point I promised earlier. Writing, and how that could catapult your sales and transform prospects to clients or customers.

3) It is written

Do your best to bring a notepad and pen with you at every meeting you attend. Why? This allows you to remember the important parts of the conversation. This will also allow you to transition between questions because you would have written context to refer to.

Before you go and think, "Will every meeting need this?" the answer to that is a resounding "Yes!" You will notice that meetings often have written minutes. That document keeps people accountable. Going into a meeting or leaving one without having minutes noted will leave most people clueless about the next steps. What you note down in the initial meeting is what would be used in your follow-up interactions with the prospect.

Some think they are too 'cool' to write and think they will remember later. The longest memory cannot compete with the shortest of pencils.

I once had the privilege of sitting with the CEO of a large company. In that meeting, she mentioned how frustrated she was with the person that she previously dealt with. Being the curious person that I am; I asked questions to find out what frustrated her. She mentioned that the previous sales consultant never wrote anything down in any of their meetings, despite her insistence on this. This led to him presenting solutions that were way off the mark as the solutions did not tie up with what that the CEO needed. Her frustration caused her to look for other people who could deliver the solution. I happily fell under the "other people" category. As she was complaining you can guess what I was doing: writing it all down.

That sales consultant will keep losing business if he never rectifies his problem of not writing things down.

Watch out for this...

I also know from experience how weird it is when I am writing something down and the prospect gives me a look that says, "Just listen, no need to write." Do not fold under such pressure.

Remember what I said about how all salespeople are leaders? Leaders do not fold when they know their actions are for the betterment of all those involved. Let the prospect know that you will be taking down notes and that it is in their best interest for you to do so. I am yet to hear a prospect say no to this when they know it is in their best interest.

My next point may be obvious, but my mind is telling me it is worth mentioning. The notepad that you bring should be clean, and the pen that you use should be one that can write. If your notepad and pen are branded with your company logo, then that is even better. This speaks volumes about your brand and your level of professionalism.

Do not forget the contract...

Apart from the compulsory notepad and pen, bring a contract too or ensure that you can conclude the sale immediately if the buying signs are imminent.

The action of bringing a contract could do two things for your prospect. It makes them decide right there and then, which would save both of you time and money. If you have followed the previous chapters well, the chances of them signing are remarkably high. Secondly, this would allow your prospect to let go of the pain they have been experiencing without your solution. I have had situations where the prospect would blatantly ask, "So, where do I sign?" and when I did not have the paperwork ready, I eventually lost the sale. Do not do what I did. Be prepared.

Before you ask them to sign, ensure that you summarise the problem they have and the solution you are providing. Confirm that you have adequately captured what was discussed. If you have a contract, get them to sign that immediately. If not, then ensure you send them an invoice with the payment date that you would have agreed to.

Please take note that all of this is happening while you are seated. Nothing has been noted while you are standing. We stand when we are done.

Recap...

1) You ought to make sure that you have written all the important points in a notepad, and that you have their permission to take note of everything. Only write what is important. Do not look at the notepad during the whole meeting. Ensure you have more eye contact with them than with the notepad. Remember you are primarily there to connect.

2) Secondly, have some sort of contract ready for them to commit to if all the buying signs present themselves. Do not waste any more time thinking that you will email it later. Let them leave that meeting knowing that there is one less thing for them to deal with. The faster you can do this, the more you will be admired and re-hired.

Do you have a contract? Do you have a quick invoicing system? Do you have a branded and clean notepad with a pen that works?

So, what next?

You can now connect with your prospect which has allowed you to convert them to your client and customer. Let us look into the first aspect of increasing your sales exponentially, public speaking!

CHAPTER 12
PROPOSALS TO LARGE AUDIENCES

After pitching your service or product to a prospect, they may think to themselves, "Hey, wait a minute. I would like you to present this to my team." When this happens, smile. This is the equivalent of having a lot of meetings at once. This opportunity is golden.

At the beginning of this book, I mentioned my meeting with a large group of people at NBC. That was a golden opportunity. I believe a mistake I made, apart from terrible objection handling, was to not have sharpened my public speaking skills. If my skills had been sharpened; I would have probably earned some money from that interaction.

How would you rate your public speaking ability on a scale of 1-10? If you said anything below 11 then there is some work to do.

Speaking in front of a large audience is different from just talking to one person. I know you may think that is obvious, but it is worth taking note of some idiosyncrasies. Here are some of the differences that I have noticed.

1. You are relaying your idea to more than one person

You convey your message to more individuals which provides more chances of buy-in. You also have the stage to yourself and do not have to deal with objections. Everyone will usually listen for the duration of your sale. This allows you to go through your full presentation instead of breaking in between. Just ensure you understand what objections people would usually have, and address these in your presentation.

2. You are more persuasive

The number one fear in the world is public speaking. People would rather be in a coffin than relaying a message in front of a group of people. By merely standing up in front of people you already display a sense of authority and courage. To ensure that you do not lose that, you need to make sure that your message is airtight. By airtight, I mean that your facts are up to date and your slides or visual aids are impeccable. If there is a question and answer session built within your presentation, you should close that session off with a summary to ensure that you are the last voice heard.

How do you present in front of a crowd?

1. How much time do you have?

All presentations begin here. If you do not know how much time you have, then you would need to find that out upfront.

Once you have confirmed your allotted time, the next step would be to cut that presentation into thirds. The first two-thirds are about relaying your information. The last third, depending on the size of the audience, would be to go through a question and answer session. You could mix it up further by relaying some information and getting the audience to ask questions right after the information is relayed. Whatever the case, ensure that you have some interaction. It allows you to know that the information is understood and that the audience is still alive.

Write out the full presentation and then master it. Every 130 words written roughly equate to 1 minute of speaking. The point here is not to repeat it verbatim; but rather to know how to transition between slides and different sets of information. Knowing your presentation also allows you to focus on the most important people – the audience. The more confident you are about your presentation, the better you can focus on your audience.

If you are using slides, you should aim to have more pictures than words. Your pictures could have minimal words on them, but that is the secret right there. It must be minimal. You also need to have mastered your slides so well that you do not need to look at them. You just need to look at the audience and wow them.

2. A call to action

Remember that the only reason you are standing in front of people is that you have a solution that can help them. Every word you put towards your presentation needs to speak to that.

Once you have completed your presentation, there must be a call to action. This is the most important part. If you miss this, you have just relayed information with no cause.

When I started in sales, I did not have a call to action and this became a problem after presentations. The only reaction I would get from an audience walking out would be, "Thank you for the presentation, it was insightful." You do not want that. Ensure that you let people know what to do after your presentation. Let them know how they could take their decision further. They need to know the process thereafter. If not, they walk out, and you do not make a sale.

To further add to this thought; make sure you have an attendance register circulating the room. This will ensure that you can follow up with interested parties. Circulating this beforehand would be great because there might be limited time after a presentation.

I once delivered a speech to an audience about how to turn your speech into a book. I presented a 20-minute talk. Once it was done, I had no way to follow up with the interested people and this came back to bite me. Some people had travelled specifically for this presentation and for me to not have capitalised on it was an injustice for me and for the people that took time to attend. I have since learnt from that presentation and always have an order sheet with me or an email subscription option. As I improve, so will the way I obtain information from the audience.

Do the right thing. Inform your audience about what to do next.

Lastly, I would like to share the structure I use to achieve buy-in through presentations.

1. State the problem and how it relates to the audience.
2. State what has been tried and why it has failed.
3. State what works, have data and share a few quotes from other experts (optional).
4. Give a success story.
5. Show how it applies to them.
6. Close the presentation by heading into questions and answers session.
7. Summarise and give a call to action.

Weave through those elements and you will have an audience that wants what you have to offer.

Recap...

There will be a time when you stand in front of a large audience and present your solutions. When this happens, you need not buckle under the pressure or worse, say no to the opportunity. Rather agree, then head to the drawing board. Write out the full presentation and follow the structure that I have just detailed. Master the presentation and go out there and deliver.

If you do that well, you will get sales.

If you would like to fast-track that process then ask to present to your prospect's team, society, or family; depending on the product/service that you are offering.

So, what next?

You now have the mechanisms to speak to a large audience. Are you done with your sale? No. You have just started a new journey; the most important one. This is where the exponential growth begins.

DURING THE SALE
CONCLUSION

You connect during the sale. This is when you listen and figure out whether your product/service is a match for the prospect(s). You also watch your prospect's body language and focus on the words they use to express their ideas.

As you write these things down, remember the Question Loop© to ensure maximum buy-in when you get to closing the deal.

Objections will surface here and there but that is part of the sales process. Remember, listen and understand what the objection pertains to before answering. Also, remember that you are more knowledgeable in these interactions and therefore, the more persuasive of the two of you. Use this power with integrity. It is not about reaching your quota; it is about fulfilling a need and ensuring that you have a quality client or customer with your product/service.

Finally, ask for the sale!

AFTER
THE SALE

If you can make one sale then well done to you. If, however, you can make more sales with the same prospect then you are onto something. The sales process is not just about that one sale; it is about keeping that client for as long as you can. It is about identifying his/her future needs and then providing a solution. This will ensure that you keep a pipeline of business that will benefit you going forward.

This also allows you to keep your acquisition costs low. It takes a lot of time and money to acquire a new client. It is in your best interest to ensure that you keep them on your books for as long as possible.

I was a waiter at a restaurant called Cappuccinos and like all restaurants, if you serve your customer well, you get rewarded with a tip. If your patrons, after paying for their bill, decide to stay for a bit longer, then you have an interesting choice. Do you offer them coffee, tea, a cold beverage, and some cake or even just water? The choice to continue to serve them could earn you extra commission simply because you went the extra mile of ensuring that they were still happy, even after their initial purchase. How can you apply that in your business?

At the end of my first book, *When the Golden Goose Doesn't Lay Eggs: Lessons on Fulfilling Your Potential*, I provide a list of other books that I plan on writing. What this does for the customer at hand is to prepare them for more. The solutions I plan to offer are endless and I am certain that they will resonate with someone who will end up buying the next set of books as well.

I am sure by now you get the point. It is awesome to get a customer. What is equally important, if not more important, is keeping that client on your books by consistently looking for more to offer them. This means that you should ensure that you know your client well enough to consistently anticipate their needs. You can do this through surveys or questionnaires that would allow you to gain more insight into the needs you could address next. Feedback forms are valuable when it comes to executing this idea because they ensure that you have a great idea of where people want to go. If you have been in your industry for a while; then you would most probably know what those needs may be.

If you, however, are still a novice in your industry, then you should think of additional items that clients may need. It is also important to ask if you are unsure. The client or customer will guide you.

In the next chapter, I will discuss how to keep in touch with your clientele or customer base. For now, answer the following question: how will your current products/services continuously be of service to your clientele or customer base?

CHAPTER 13
KEEP IN TOUCH

There are several ways of keeping in touch with your clients. Once you have made the sale and have their buy-in; the next step would be to find out more information about them.

Do you know what local sports team they support? When their birthday is? Their wedding anniversary? Their children's birthdays? The information in the news or on the internet that speaks about that person's industry? All the above information is particularly important. This is how you organically keep in touch with someone.

Organically is always more important as opposed to just calling for the sake of calling. The latter method will damage your reputation. Instead, call with the former in mind. This will propel you to stay top of mind and your client may go out of their way, at times, to be of assistance to you.

I remember selling a mass order of books to a client, as a prize for the group that I would be speaking to. When I called to find out when he would pay the invoice I sent him; I noted that he was watching cricket at the time. South Africa was playing some team (that should tell you my interest in cricket) and he wanted South Africa to win. This is all the information I needed to ensure that there was a constant connection.

The next time I called to follow up on the payment for the books, guess what I talked about? Cricket! It was important to him. It also showed that I paid attention to the details of his life and that I cared. Now each time South Africa play, I try to send him a text just to wish him well on the game. This is after he purchased my books.

People who do this consistently will grow, but very few people do this as it takes effort. You must see your customers from a long-term engagement viewpoint, which requires listening and paying attention to details. This is where what you would have written becomes remarkably important.

But I am not detail-orientated Grant...

If you have trouble with listening and paying attention to detail, then I advise that you join a Toastmasters club and learn to evaluate speeches. This is the act of hearing your speaker's speech then providing them with feedback on it. The people who are great at it can pick out bits and pieces of your speech and tell you what you did exceedingly well and what you ought to improve on. To do this well you have to clear your mind and pay full attention to the speaker. This skill can be directly translated to your customer.

If you cannot join a Toastmasters club, then perhaps practise on close friends and family. While they are speaking at a function, just listen. When it is your turn to speak, try and build on the points they may have raised, but acknowledge them as you do so. Take careful note of how they will respond to you afterwards.

Keeping in touch even without the sale

I know this is not the happiest piece of advice for someone who may have missed out on the sale, but you must keep that person as part of your contacts going forward. This is still an advantage. Firstly, things change in people's lives and as they do, they could seek your advice or product to help them. Just because it did not apply to them this time around it does not mean that it will not apply to them later in life. Secondly, not everyone buys the first time you try to sell to them. Sometimes people want to see how consistent you are with your business and whether you would be able to meet their need. Your patience in this process will prove to be your biggest ally. I forget the source, but I remember reading how 60% to 80% of sales are not immediate. The rejections during this period only require you to be patient and keep asking instead. The 20% to 40% of immediate purchases may be awesome at the beginning, but that is only the tip of the iceberg. There is still more you could obtain.

I believe it is the true mark of a salesperson that, despite receiving a no, we are still able to keep in contact with that person. This reveals that you do not take things personally.

I remember our regional manager speaking at a sales conference at my previous job. He had previous experience in the financial advisory space and was a manager elsewhere before being appointed regional manager. He mentioned that he never let go of a contact at his previous workplace. He understood the importance of regularly keeping in touch with contacts and keeping up with the changes in their lives. This helped as he was top of mind when the customer was in a place where they could finally purchase what he was offering. This added a lot of income that would have otherwise been lost had he thrown away that contact.

Never let go of the contacts you meet as you begin to sell your products/services. Never see them as once-off contacts because these are people that have taken the time to see you. You just need to remain top of mind, even if they have not purchased at this point. If they tell you, "Maybe now is not the time" your response should be, "So, when would it suit you to have this discussion again?" Wait for the answer, note it down then follow through. You will be shocked at how many people would say yes to a sale when asked a second time.

Remember Mark Chivere from earlier on, who owns a company that deals with behaviour tests and helping brands with their strategies? I remember him mentioning to me how he called a prominent brand and asked if he could come in to deliver a presentation. They said, "No, not right now. Call me a year later at this time and we can take it from there." The person who told him that may have thought, "Well, I sure got rid of him now." But no, my friend sent him a meeting request for a year later at the time the manager had specified.

A year later, that manager is sitting at his computer screen and a meeting reminder pops up. As he begins to smile thinking that the meeting was not taking place, he hears his phone ring. On that day Mark was able to close a deal worth a lot of money simply because he kept the contact and followed through a year later.

Whose name did you throw away because they said no to you? In future, I would recommend that you keep that contact. It will come in handy one day, and even if they do not, then you would still be at the same place you were when they said no to you the first time. Why not take that chance?

Recap...

Sale or no sale, keeping in touch is the key to more sales as it will keep you relevant in the lives of those you have sold to or are yet to sell to. Not doing this will keep your sales linear, and thereafter it could come to a halt. If you want exponential growth though, keeping the contact should be part of your arsenal.

So, what next?

Exponential growth begins with keeping the connection. The second step is referrals. Let us chat a bit about that.

CHAPTER 14
REFERRALS

Sometimes the people we meet with might be the wrong people to talk to. They may not need our product/service, or their finances may not allow them to purchase from us. In times like these, I want you to do something that a few people would dare to do: ask for referrals. That person may have not given you the business but may know someone who could. Why not replace them with more contacts that could land you the business?

Who else can I help?

At this point, you would have built enough trust to ask this person for a referral or referrals. When you do this, remember that the contacts they give you are privy to you. That prospect trusts you so treat their contacts like gold and do not break that trust. Also, ensure that you get back to the referee for every one of the referrals they provided. Why? Because they would appreciate the recognition if all goes well and will be noted as helpful because of it. If, however, it does not work out, then most referees would give you a new list to work with.

The general rule with referrals is that you call them five minutes after their details were given to you. They are still fresh by then and you still have the enthusiasm of having received them. This would allow your enthusiasm to greet them, therefore, a meeting would be more likely.

If you do not want to contact them immediately or cannot; then perhaps ask the referee to contact them. To make this successful, ensure you provide a simple two-line script for the referee to use as they contact the referrals. This would help the referee prime their contacts for your call. The referrals would then be expecting your call and be more open to your proposals.

Growth of Network

Ever heard the phrase, "Your network is your net worth." The exercise that would follow this phrase is to get you to figure out the average salary of your five closest friends and see how close your salary is to that average. I believe it to be true. You can only go as far as your network allows and when this happens then you have the choice to go into other networks that may be more beneficial to yours. Do not feel bad for leaving your network to find one that may be more beneficial. This is because of the growth you are pursuing. It is nothing personal.

I joined Toastmasters a few years ago and that has opened my network to more people than the usual church events that I would go to. This has also allowed me to view things differently and has drastically helped my business.

When I had my first book launch, most of the people who attended were Toastmasters. They have been avidly supporting my book through sales since then. This is the power of expanding your current network.

The question now is: how do you grow your network? Figure out the ideal people that would buy your product/service and ask yourself where you would find these people. Start to position yourself within those crowds as it will open a new world to you, and a new set of customers.

Did someone say collaborate?

As you meet possible candidates to financially support your cause, you will find people that could be worth more to you. You will find people that will not only buy but be able to take your products or services to a larger group of people. You need to recognise someone like this as soon as possible. You will only be able to see such a person by understanding who they are and how influential they may be.

What will also help you identify this person would be the number of products/services you would have sold to them. If you have sold your product/service to that individual more than once, then chances are high that they could give you a referral or collaborate with you to find new markets.

When I realised that some individuals bought more books than others, I began to build a relationship with them. A relationship is when you are mutually beneficial to each other. You can help them, and they can help you and you are both willing to do so. If the criteria are not met, then no relationship could form. If they are willing to help you and you are not able to help them, then having them help you repeatedly may become draining for them. If you can help them and they cannot help you, then you would have to think of ways they could assist. I am not saying you go tit-for-tat. What I am saying is that a relationship should benefit both of you.

If anything, I would always advise that you are doing more for people than they are doing for you. This allows you to enter the grounds of possibly getting help as well. Be genuine though, no one likes to be helped by someone who is always seeking a favour afterwards. That is just being manipulative.

Ultimately, collaboration ensures that your network grows, which ensures that you are exposed to more people. As Grant Cardone always says, "Obscurity is the number one problem of entrepreneurs."

Get out there, meet new people and collaborate.

Massive goals or dreams have never been achieved by one person. It was Jesse Jackson that said, "We stand on the shoulders of those before us." The same goes for you. For you to get more exposure and better relevance with those that are around, you need people to expose your product/service.

Ideas anyone?

The other advantage of this will be getting more ideas. As we communicate with people, we are ultimately selling ideas.

When I began writing my first book, I thought to myself, "How will I get a punchy title?" Initially, my book title was: *When Potential is not Enough: 3 Steps to Achieving Your Potential.* After some time though, that idea slowly began to act like milk that had been left out in the open for too long. It was only after listening to a podcast series that I heard someone mention that people see things in images and that is what reels them in. The next challenge was how do I reel people in? How do I draw a picture in their minds to let them know that they have an ocean depth of potential but are doing nothing about it? The gentleman in that series then alluded to a book that I love called, *"The tall lady with the glass."* This book speaks about the power of metaphors and how they draw pictures in people's minds. BINGO! I needed to use a metaphor and perhaps a picture that would exemplify this. Did this all come together immediately? No! The title first came as, "When the Golden Goose Doesn't Lay Golden Eggs." But that was repetitive so I took off the "golden" because golden geese could only lay golden eggs. Next, I looked at my subtitle. Someone said that I cannot call it steps and that I should rather view it as lessons because life does not consist of steps – it is not perfectly aligned. You move from one point to another in a more complex fashion. "Rather say lessons, Grant, and allow the audience to grasp what they would need to get."

Thus, the subtitle, "Lessons on fulfilling your potential". Then came the idea of the goose on the cover. Now that I had an awesome title, I needed to reflect it in an image so that people understand that the goose is golden and has a boundless amount of potential, but for some reason does not live up to it. That was easy enough.

As a result, I speak to numerous people about an idea before I act on it. Try it because your ideas will only take you so far; the ideas of others will ensure that you can go farther. Much farther than you would have had you decided to just go by yourself. Why is this so? Because people see things differently and will see something that you may not. By understanding this, you are then able to implement an idea that would surpass you and get you an audience of people you would have otherwise never met.

I connect people...

As you meet all these different people, remember to keep their details. Sometimes you may meet people who have a problem that your product or service does not address yet. Instead of disregarding these people, you can link them up with someone who can help them. You will be viewed as helpful, honest, and considerate. This may not pay off in the short term. However, as you spend time connecting others; you would also get to widen your network. As you connect, ask to also be connected or referred to someone else.

In a world where people tend to be stingy with their contacts; be that one person who decides to share. It will come back to you twofold.

Recap...

Referrals are vital to growing your business. Ask for them and follow up by contacting them. Take the time to intentionally grow your network because the more people you sell to, the higher the chances for more sales. Learn to listen to the ideas that are out there as they will lead you to develop better ways of selling or producing your products/services. Lastly, do not keep all the people you are connecting with to yourself. Learn to share them with people you have qualified.

If you can intentionally do all the above, your sales will grow exponentially.

So, what next?

Time to conclude our time together as you need to apply what you can and begin to grow your sales exponentially. So, let us wrap this up.

AFTER THE SALE
CONCLUSION

You can produce sales without using the strategies presented in this section. However, if you are looking to grow sales exponentially, then using these strategies will be of better value to you. Keeping in touch with those you meet is important; whether they have bought from you or not.

I would advise you to get a customer relationship management (CRM) system. It should help to distinguish those who have bought from you and those that have not. This will keep your pipeline full of leads which means you won't have to start with zero customers every month.

Learn to ask for referrals and add these people to the CRM. Follow up with them as soon as possible.

Remember, this is where the money is. Every activity that got you here was merely a start.

CHAPTER 15
LET'S WRAP THIS UP!

Sales need not be hard, dreadful or draining. Everything I have shared with you can make the process simpler and help you to achieve exponential sales.

Just remember the activities that you need to do before the sale, during the sale, and after the sale. If you do this then sales will be something you end up admiring and want to repeat.

I was once terrible at sales but now my circles tell me how great I am at it. I even had business owners asking me to train their staff. That was one of the reasons I decided to pen down what worked for me. I can promise you that I am no different from you. You can do the same too if you honour the dream to sell well by doing the necessary work.

If you need help...

If you need further guidance, we can be reached at info@thegoldengooseinstitute.com. Apart from our sales presentations and coaching, we also have a behavioural test that allows you to understand your selling style. In doing so, you can work on your strengths while hiring someone else to take care of your weaknesses. Alternatively, you could also learn how to improve your weaknesses. The point is that you would make an informed decision that would result in exponential growth. If you are in human resources, the same behavioural tests could be used to gain the right personnel to hire because it is better to not have a problem, to begin with, than to look for solutions towards one. Let us get you started on a process that will change your life or your company's.

If we do not meet again, I implore you to go out there with your products/services and make the world a better place. The world is waiting.

ABOUT THE AUTHOR

Grant Senzani strongly believes in your potential and how you can actualize anything and everything you desire to become. His mantra is, "We honour the dream, by doing the work".

He is a Distinguished Toastmaster, professional speaker, author of three books, and a certified life and body coach. He is also a certified neuro-linguistic practitioner.

He shares easy, yet very productive ways on how to become a successful seller whether you are an entrepreneur or form part of a sales team in corporate.

If you are looking to excel and make your dreams or targets tangible; book him and his team at info@thegoldengooseinstitute.com we guarantee we will not only recognize the problem, but we will solve it too and ensure your results are sustainable over the long haul.

Lastly, you can also connect with him and the team by listening to https://open.spotify.com/show/0ELb22kZc2taYT76F0o1lZ

Grant looks forward to hearing from you and being of service to you.

www.ingramcontent.com/pod-product-compliance
Lightning Source LLC
Chambersburg PA
CBHW020155200326
41521CB00006B/377